Research
nts

SSUE

PROBLEM-SOLVING
THROUGH CREATIVE ANALYSIS

Problem-solving through Creative Analysis

TUDOR RICKARDS

A Gower Press Special Study

First published in Great Britain by Gower Press Limited, Epping, Essex 1974

ISBN 0 7161 0214 5

Typeset by H Charlesworth & Co Ltd, Huddersfield
Printed in England by Lowe & Brydone (Printers) Ltd, Thetford

Contents

Illustrations

Foreword

The last decade has seen another upsurge of interest in creativity as a potentially important management function. My own interest was stimulated about six years ago while working for Unilever Research Ltd (UK), on the development of new products. I eventually joined a specialist group which had been one of the first exponents of creativity-spurring techniques in groups in this country. In addition to using techniques on real problems I was provided with opportunities for teaching them in Unilever groups, in the UK and other countries, and also with time to examine the general theory behind their application.

In common with other similar groups we found that textbooks were useful up to a point but glossed over several key areas of difficulty – for example, the procedures to be adopted to ensure that an idea got the best chance of being progressed through the organization. Such problems led us to adapt a healthy empiricism, selecting elements from various sources to make up our problem-solving armoury. At the same time other groups with which we were in contact, starting from similar reference materials and techniques, developed quite different systems of problem-solving. In retrospect it could be seen that the groups were making a creative analysis – selecting and modifying techniques according to their needs.

Later I presented my experiences in a series of management seminars at Manchester Business School. The theme of the seminars in 1972–73 was 'fresh inputs to innovation: the role of creative techniques' and from discussions with participants in a variety of managerial environments an approach to problem-solving crystallized which was called creative analysis. It has since been tested in consultancy situations as INCA – Innovation through Creative Analysis.

There have been one or two encouraging successes for INCA, including the invention of new-product concepts for two different companies and a few patented ideas. However, the main justification for presenting the body of theory and practical experience in a text lies in its apparent wide applicability. Aspects have been found relevant to such diverse audiences as mathematical modelling units, HM prison governors, engineering faculties, the OR Society, basic research teams, new-product groups, advertising agencies, technologists and social workers.

I hope the reader, too, will find elements suitable to his own particular work environment.

Acknowledgements

I should like to thank Unilever Ltd for experience gained over the period 1967–71, and especially to colleagues in New Products Concepts section at Port Sunlight, and Dr Michael Woods at Colworth House.

At Manchester Business School a stimulating atmosphere and practical assistance came from the faculty and in particular Alan Pearson and members of his research unit into R and D management. At Gower Press, Penelope Lloyd's suggestions led me to clarify my own thinking on a variety of points. Industrial managers and clients always seemed to give me at least as many insights as I was able to provide them in discussing creative problem-solving. Only a few of these people are mentioned in the text and I can only hope that I have not distorted their views in the process of describing them.

In preparing the first draft of the manuscript Jane West became a very competent practitioner of some of the techniques and contributed to the seminars involving them. The final draft was prepared by Liz Calligan and her team at C.S.S. who coped with increasingly urgent deadlines. Under pressure for even longer was my wife who must have developed her own problem-solving techniques to preserve a tolerant attitude during the year between incubation and formulation of the final manuscript.

PART ONE

THE TECHNIQUES OF CREATIVE ANALYSIS

Chapter 1

Introduction to Creative Analysis

1.1 *SCOPE AND FORMAT OF THE BOOK*

The objective of this book is to help managers tackle problems which can have no logically correct answer (open-ended problems) and which tend to require the controlled use of creativity-spurring techniques. The overall framework for assimilating effective procedures is termed 'creative analysis'.

The book has been written for managers whose responsibilities include dealing with and solving open-ended problems ranging from reducing global pollution to inventing brand names for new products. Creative analysis has been practised by individuals and groups in research laboratories, advertising agencies, corporate strategy units, market research groups, OR/management science departments, think tanks, technical divisions and various other industrial, public and academic environments.

In Chapter 1 creative analysis is introduced in the context of five main classes of techniques. These are shown in Figure 1:1 together with their subroutines. The *subroutines* are specific techniques or elements within a technique which can be introduced, modified, and generally juxtaposed within a manager's developing system. It is because of this flexibility that creative analysis becomes possible. In the following chapters the actual techniques are described. Chapters 2 to 4 deal with aids which are most often employed by the individual

Figure 1:1 Problem-solving techniques and their subroutines

Techniques for individual problem-solving		*Techniques for group problem-solving*	
Class T.1	Restructuring techniques	Class T.4	Brainstorming
T.1.1	Morphological analysis	T.4.1	Osborn's methods
T.1.2	Relevance systems	T.4.2	Trigger sessions
T.1.3	Attribute lists	T.4.3	Recorded round robin ('6–3–5')
T.1.4	Research planning diagrams	T.4.4	Wildest idea
		T.4.5	Reverse brainstorming
Class T.2	Decision aids	T.4.6	Individual brainstorming*
T.2.1	Weighting procedures		
T.2.2	Checklists	Class T.5	Synectics
Class T.3	Redefinitional aids	T.5.1	Active listening/constructive group behaviour
T.3.1	Goal orientation	T.5.2	Goal orientation
T.3.2	Successive abstractions	T.5.3	Itemization
T.3.3	Analogy procedures	T.5.4	Changed meeting roles
T.3.4	Wishful thinking	T.5.5	Excursion procedures (speculation and analogy)
T.3.5	Nonlogical stimuli	T.5.6	Individual synectics*
T.3.6	Boundary examinations		
T.3.7	Reversals		

The classification of techniques and subroutines within the main classes will be used as identifiers elsewhere.

*Although known and tested, these subroutines are rather unusual in practice, and are not considered further.

problem-solver and these are followed in Chapters 5 and 6 by brainstorming and synectics, two systems of techniques particularly suited to group activities. I will discuss later why groups should play an important part in managerial problem-solving. Chapter 7 recapitulates on the principles whereby the techniques might be assimilated into practice, illustrating the point with a series of actual problems. In Chapters 8 to 12 (Part Two) a series of case studies is presented illustrating the use of the techniques and/or of creative analysis. As the reader experiments with the methods described in Part One he will be able to compare his experience with the accounts given in Part Two.

Figures 1:2 and 1:3 are cross-reference tables which give details of current and possible additional applications of the techniques by the type of management group involved (Figure 1:2), and details of the techniques and management environments described in each of the case studies (Figure 1:3). The tables are intended to highlight existing possibilities, and to suggest to the reader potential new applications within his own organization.

1.2 THE TECHNIQUES AND THEIR SUBROUTINES

Five main categories of technique are described in the following chapters. They are:

1	Restructuring techniques (Chapter 2)	Mostly used by the individual problem-solver
2	Decision aids (Chapter 3)	
3	Redefinitional procedures (Chapter 4)	
4	Brainstorming (Chapter 5)	Mostly used in group activities as described
5	Synectics-type procedures (Chapter 6)	

Restructuring techniques

Some problems are so complex that they need to be displayed systematically before they can be understood properly. Typical examples occur in product design – for example, considering possibilities for a new type of wheeled tray, or a carpet cleaner or a toothbrush. *Morphological analysis* could be used for these problems.

Relevance systems are used for situations in which there is a need to examine relationships, either within an area, or between two interrelated areas. A single relevance tree can represent a broad programme or policy in terms of less complex aspects. A binary relevance system can show the relationships (or lack of them) between two complex and interrelated areas such as a company's long-term objectives and its basic research programme.

For restructuring dynamic situations *attribute lists* have been found effective, while as an extension of the computer logic systems *research planning diagrams* have much to commend them.

In general the restructuring techniques do not solve a problem completely, but represent it in a way which makes its solution (by application of other techniques) easier.

Figure 1:2 *Current and potential use of the techniques in various management environments*

Environments	Techniques: Restructuring aids T.1				Decision aids T.2		Redefinitional aids T.3							Brainstorming T.4						Synectics T.5				
	T.1.1	T.1.2	T.1.3	T.1.4	T.2.1	T.2.2	T.3.1	T.3.2	T.3.3	T.3.4	T.3.5	T.3.6	T.3.7	T.4.1	T.4.2	T.4.3	T.4.4	T.4.5	T.4.6	T.5.1	T.5.2	T.5.3	T.5.4	T.5.5
Advertising agencies	○				●	●							○	○		○	○	○			○		○	○
Corporate strategy units		○			○	○														●	●	●		
Engineering	○		○		○	○					●	●		○	○					●	●	●		
Individual junior managers							●	●	●	●	●	●		○			●	●		●	●	●	●	●
Individual middle managers	○	○	○	○	○	○	○	○	○	○	○	○	○	○	○	○	○	○	○	○	○	○	○	○
Individual senior managers	○	○				○						●							●	●	○		○	○
Invention groups	○	○			○	○		○	○	○	○	○		○	○	○	○	○		○	○	○	○	○
Market research groups	○		○		○	○			○	○	○		○	○		○	●	○	○	○	○		○	○
OR/Management science groups	○	○	○	○	○	○						○		○			○	○	○	○	○		○	○
Product managers	●	●	○	●		○	●	●	●	●	●	●		○					●		○		○	○
Production departments				○	○	●	●	●	●	●	●	○		○	○			○			○		○	○
Personnel counselling					●					○	○		●	○						○	○	○	○	○
Public service administrators						●				●	●	●		○						●	●	●		
Technical managers	○			○	○	○	○	○	●	●	●	○		○	○	○	○	○		○	○	○	○	○
Think tanks	○	○			○	○	●	●	●	●	●	●		○	●	●	●	●		○	○	○	●	●
Training departments				●	○	○		○		○	○			○						●	○	●	○	○
Value analysis	○		○		○	○				●		●		○	○	●	●	○			○		○	○
Venture groups	○	○	○			○						●		●						●	○	●	○	○

Key
- ○ Subroutine known to be applicable in the given environment
- ● Subroutine thought to be potentially applicable in the given environment

T.1.1, etc. See Figure 1:1 for key to the various subroutines

Figure 1:3 *Techniques used in the case studies.*
Excluding the individual activities, Case Studies 19–23.

Case study	*Type of group involved*	*Restructuring techniques*	*Decision aids*	*Redefinitional techniques*	*Brainstorming (various)*	*Synectics (various)*
1	Invention group; engineering client					✓
2	Invention group; market research	✓	✓		✓	✓
3	Invention group; technical group				✓	✓
4	Invention group; training department	✓			✓	✓
5	OR group; process problems	✓	✓	✓	✓	
6	New-business group; outside consultant				✓	✓
7	Training department				✓	
8	Inventions group; outside consultant				✓	
9	Market research group	✓		✓		
10	Market research group plus consumer				✓	✓
11	Technical group plus consumer					✓
12	Market research plus consumer					✓
13	Market research plus consumer					✓
14	Inventions group				✓	
15	Training department				✓	
16	Inventions group				✓	
17	Think tanks				✓	
18	Market research plus consumer				✓	

Decision aids

The mathematical procedures for aiding decisions have been well documented, and only two of the most robust and simple to operate are included here. These are *weighting procedures*, in which the analyst attributes numerical figures to the factors within the decision area; and *checklists* which are useful guides to avoid overlooking one or more elements which need to be included in the decision-making process.

Redefinitional procedures

Successful solvers of open-ended problems have developed an ability to maintain a flexible attitude to defining problems. As a result they are in a good position to accept suggestions which make them alter their earlier definitions – that is, suggestions which change their view of the boundaries of problems. (Incidentally, once a problem redefinition is accepted the solution becomes 'obvious' to many people who had not been able to arrive at the solution previously.)

A variety of forces operate which produce mental blocks towards problem redefinition: overcommitment to a certain line of approach, excessive logic, unwillingness to speculate, excessive deference towards accepted 'expert' views and so on. A variety of aids to overcome these blocks are known and I have called them redefinitional aids. For example *goal orientation* and *boundary examinations* help clarify the boundaries which have to be accepted and those which can be usefully challenged. *Successive abstractions, metaphor, random stimuli,* and *reversals* help break away from convenience and rigid thinking.

Group idea-generation and problem-solving techniques

The two most popular classes of group techniques are *brainstorming* and *synectics*. An attempt is made to represent them with the minimum of jargon in Chapters 5 and 6. Each is essentially a system of elements or subroutines which can be introduced in differing order and substituted for one another. Creative analysis is used to adapt group techniques for use. In other words, the subroutines are the core elements out of which one can extract a system which helps one to solve particular problems. Just how this is done is the subject of the next section.

1.3 CREATIVE ANALYSIS

A *creative analysis* of a problem situation is an attempt to solve it in a way which links one's own experience with generally accepted principles for tackling similar types of problem.

Although, theoretically, creative analysis can be applied to most problems it operates best in circumstances which cannot be rigorously defined – described above as open-ended problem situations.

In essence creative analysis is a process of learning from experience. It is illustrated by Figure 1:4, which represents a sequence of problem-

Figure 1:4 Creative analysis demonstrating the incorporation of techniques and modifications as a result of learning

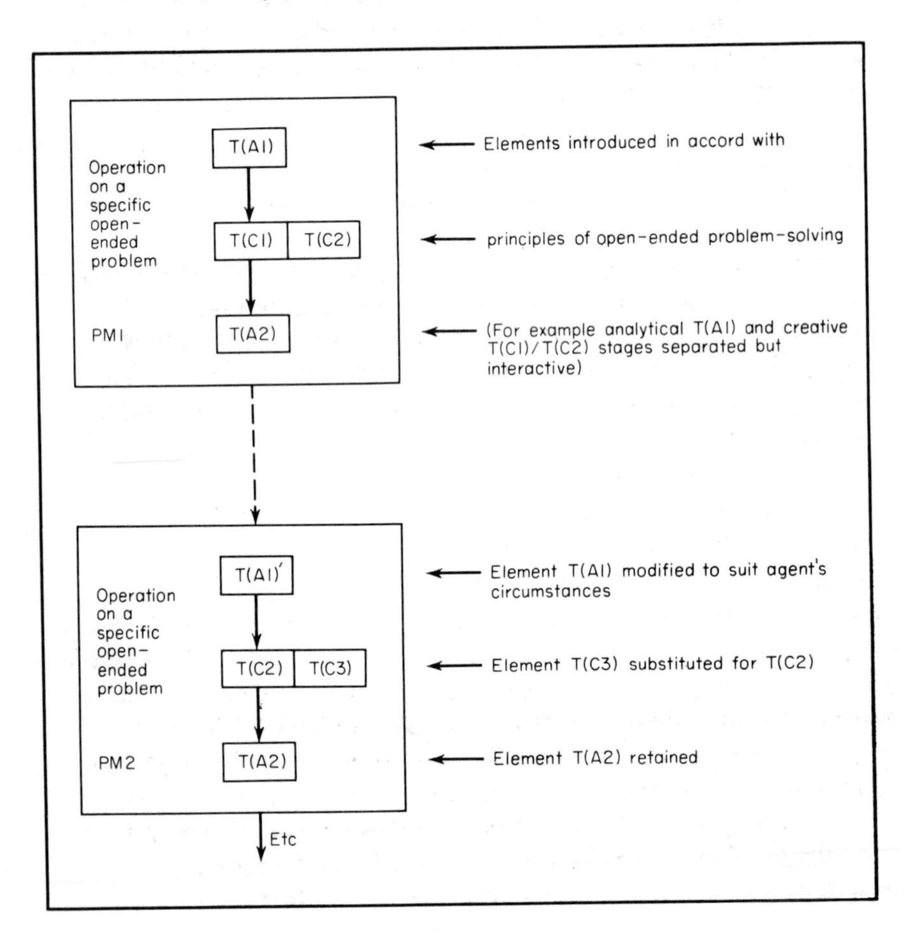

solving procedures. The first problem (PM1) is tackled in three stages: an analytical technique, two creative techniques and a second analytical technique. The solver is already using an awareness of some underlying principles of tackling this sort of problem by keeping the creative and analytical stages separate but interacting.

As a result of his experience the problem-solver will be better equipped in future to tackle problems which appear to have similar characteristics. In this example he modifies the first analytical procedure and replaces one creative technique with a different one. Each problem becomes a learning experience which enables him to develop his own problem-solving style.

Some of the techniques are sufficiently complex to represent a valid system for creative analysis on their own. This particularly applies to brainstorming and synectics – under each generic heading is a series of subroutines which can be tested, modified and adapted to use in any specific environment.

1.4 PRINCIPLES UNDERLYING CREATIVE ANALYSIS

When someone uses a technique for problem-solving he is well advised to appreciate the principles and theories underlying it. Most of the principles of the techniques described have widespread acceptance but it is still important for the problem-solver to relate them to his own circumstances. Four main categories of assumptions are made, relating respectively to:

1 The nature of open-ended problems
2 Problem-solving roles and sphere of influence
3 Creative and analytical processes
4 Individual and group problem-solving

Open-ended problems

An open-ended solving situation exists if a problem has been recognized and the solver believes that he can usefully challenge one or more of its boundary conditions.

The less he is prepared to challenge the boundaries the less open-ended the problem is – as far as he is concerned. In school we are often in positions of a strictly close-ended nature (there is not much point asking why we are 'given a straight line tangential to a circle' or why we have to establish whether Socrates was or was not human).

Unfortunately the educational experience seems to contribute towards some people's reluctance to challenge boundaries afterwards and so they rarely recognize situations as potentially open-ended. Many managers work to such rigid time constraints that for practical purposes they appear justified in treating their problems as close-ended. For example, a manager with responsibility for maintaining a production target is often too busy to stop and examine the validity of the target. But production methods and targets do change from time to time and somebody has to treat the problem as an open-ended one eventually.

Figure 1:5 demonstrates the distinction between the two types of situation. An appreciation that a situation is open-ended means that the problem-solver is also prepared to consider new approaches, to countenance new ideas outside the bounds of logic – in short to look to creative thinking to help him (Figure 1:6). The redefinitional aids of Chapter 3 and the creativity-spurring aids of Chapters 5 and 6 then become possible candidates for contributing towards the solving process.

Figure 1:5 Characteristics of open and close problem situations

Open	*Close*
Boundaries may change during problem-solving	Boundaries are fixed during problem-solving
Process of solving often involves production of novel and unexpected ideas	Process marked by predictability of final solution
Process may involve creative thinking of an uncontrollable kind	Process usually conscious, controllable and logically reconstructable
Solutions often outside the bounds of logic – can neither be proved nor disproved	Solutions often provable, logically correct
Direct (conscious) efforts at stimulation of creative process to solve problems is difficult	Procedures are known which directly aid problem-solving (algorithms or heuristics)

Figure 1:6 *Recognition of open-ended problem situations.*
Most everyday problems have some constraints or boundaries which are mistakenly assumed to be fixed. Pure close-ended problems are rarer than might be thought.

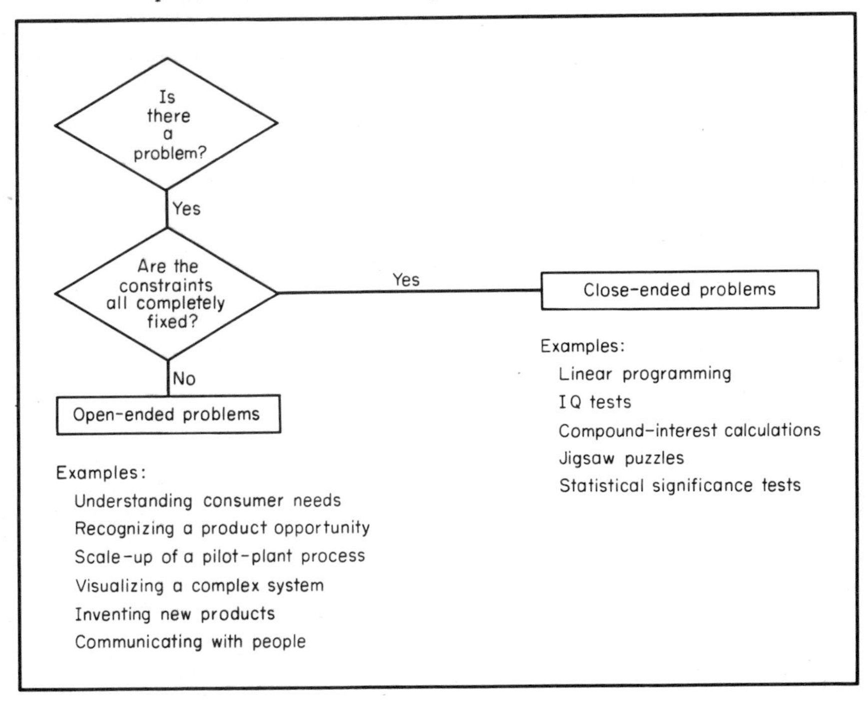

Problem-solving roles and sphere of influence

For effective creative analysis an awareness of different roles in problem-solving is important. It is possible to identify three general types of role which people can adopt (Figure 1:7):

1 The agent role
2 The group leader role
3 The group provider role

The *agent* role is recognized in the person who has assumed responsibility for tackling and executing a problem. There is a general tendency for an agent to want to work alone, particularly at the outset of a problem, when he is not sure how he will progress. This behaviour is reinforced in many management situations where to ask for help is to show weakness.

Figure 1:7 Problem-solving roles in creative analysis

Role	*Role description*	*Role activities*
Agent	The person with a brief or commitment to find a solution to a problem and to implement it	Individual problem-solving activities; identifying the need for involving other people in group problem-solving
Client	An agent who has approached a group for help in solving his problem	Seeking new insights and cooperation from other people
Expert (participant or client)	A person whose specialized expertise predisposes him towards certain types of solution	In problem-solving groups his activities are the same as a nonexpert participant or client
Leader	The person who conducts a group problem-solving activity	Attention to the format of the meeting while leaving the content to the rest of the group
Participants	Group members whose different backgrounds provide stimuli for new insights	Presentation of individual ways of seeing the problem

Nevertheless, there are circumstances in which an agent feels he must involve other people and operate within a group. Because of an agent's involvement with the problem, it is better that he should permit someone else, preferably without any personal interest in the problem, to act as group leader. The leader then looks after the process of problem-solving without permitting his own solutions to intrude. The group can also include providers, or participants who provide fresh insights for the agent. When an agent requests help from a problem-solving group he becomes known as a *client*, particularly in synectics terminology. (The terms are used interchangeably here, in group situations.) One reason which might prompt an agent to approach a group is a need to obtain information possessed by people from different backgrounds and experience, perhaps experts in different aspects of the problem.

Another important reason for involving a group would be if an agent believes he is unlikely to be able to execute ideas without involvement and cooperation from other people. Another way of looking at this is to regard the other people as *co-agents*, and the problem as falling within their joint sphere of influence. The co-agents, like an original agent, will be motivated to work on ideas they have helped develop so it becomes desirable, perhaps necessary, to involve them in group idea-generation and problem-solving activities.

A problem is said to be within the *sphere of influence* of a solver if he suspects he will be able to implement possible solutions without undue reliance on other people's approval and cooperation.

An example will illustrate this concept. Consider a production manager who recognizes that one of his machines is ageing rapidly. He believes that changes will be necessary. If he thinks he will be able to work out what changes are necessary, and then see that they are carried out, the problem is within his sphere of influence. On the other hand, he may need to discuss the problem with his supervisors and operatives, or he may require approval from his superior for his plans and may have to negotiate with other managers who are also dependent on the machine as part of their jobs. In all these cases the problem is not completely under his control, or within his sphere of influence. The implication is that possible solutions will have to have acceptance by other managers, who should therefore be involved in the solving process.

Creative and analytical problem-solving procedures

In general, creative thinking operates at a below-conscious, intuitive level, and analytical thinking at a conscious level. It is therefore generally assumed (and supported by experimental evidence) that the two processes should be kept separate for optimum efficiency. Thus different techniques are employed to help the different types of thinking. However, the processes are complementary in open-ended situations. Creative analysis will help a solver to establish how they can be separated and yet allowed to interact profitably.

At the simplest level there is the person who 'sleeps on a problem' before making a decision. The subconscious process will be given a chance to throw up new ideas before the evaluation stage starts.

The more complex techniques (brainstorming and synectics) introduce mechanisms to bring about the separation of the creative and analytical processes while permitting them to interact.

Creativity is a mysterious process which can give rise to heated arguments among psychologists. It is sufficient here to regard the process as one which gives rise to novel combinations of concepts which have significance to the solver or his environment.

Individual and group problem-solving

Traditionally, problems are tackled on an individual basis. Particularly when there is a need for inputs from more than one person (as described above, a frequent occurrence in many management situations), group techniques should be considered

Some potential advantages of group problem-solving are shown in Figure 1:8 along with some actual disadvantages. Brainstorming and synectics attempt to deal with all the disadvantages (of group problem-solving) with the exception of cost-benefit considerations. These can

Figure 1:8 Potential advantages and actual disadvantages of typical management problem-solving meetings

Potential advantages	*Actual disadvantages*
Individuals each bring different points of view which can stimulate ideas	Group problem-solving more costly in terms of resources, time and effort
Bringing together people is the best way of transferring ideas	Leader can use as a 'mock democratic' process to advance his own ideas
Confrontation forces recognition that certain beliefs are personal and not absolute	Experts tend to reject and ignore ideas from nonexperts
Group work can strengthen common objectives and motivation	Composition may be top-heavy with experts or managers of similar skills and experience or commitment to the problem
Group work can reduce 'not invented here' by including key personnel at genesis of ideas	Individual blocks to idea-generation still apply (for example, members still have a fear of looking foolish and are critical of their own and other people's ideas)
Problem-solving group will spend more man-hours than if an individual tackled the problem	Objectives of meeting unclear and procedures mixed (meeting oscillates between idea-generation and evaluation stages)
Group will reach a greater variety of points of view and possible solutions and will consider more daring strategies	Personality traits interfere with objective assessment of ideas

be taken into account by examining factors such as the visibility of the agent, timing, apparent difficulty of the problem, and potential value of a solution (Figure 1:9).

Figure 1:9 Organizational factors influencing a decision to hold a group problem-solving meeting on a recognized open-ended problem

Favourable factors	*Unfavourable factors*
A satisfactory agent can be identified	No satisfactory agent can be identified
The agent can outline his problem needs and the actions to be taken in progressing a solution	The agent wants a meeting just to see what might emerge
The timing is suitable. The agent has tried some obvious approaches, knows the main constraints and objections and believes that new insights could be obtained after a meeting	The timing is too early; the agent will not be able to recognize and modify elementary weaknesses in the solutions through his own inexperience. The timing is too late. The agent is committed to a highly constraining course of action which excludes new starting points
There is a reasonable probability of success from the solving activities	The meeting is a last resort of a manager who has tried everything else
The problem is of sufficient long-term consequence to justify time and resources spent, taking into account a rough probability of success. (A serious exercise could take six weeks from start to finish, and occupy three manager-weeks of actual work before implementing the ideas.)	The problem does not justify the effort

1.5 THE VALUE OF GOOD RECORD-KEEPING FOR CREATIVE ANALYSIS

In order to learn from problem-solving it is important to keep good records. A simple card-index of meetings with cards for individual participants, and problems tackled (giving details of clients, ideas obtained, action minutes) makes it easier to monitor progress of ideas and identify elements in the process which might be better modified in future exercises.

A more comprehensive record card is shown in Figure 1:10. This card is being used at present by several specialist problem-solving groups. It serves as a checklist and more important as a teaching aid to the group. For example, the performance of different leaders can be compared with the level of acceptance of procedure by the group, and with the types of idea obtained. The rate of production of ideas (most important in brainstorming) is a guide to whether the group is attaining a psychological state in which there is temporary suspension of conscious analytical judgement. This postponed judgement leads to creative ideas.

In time the records will guide the creative-analysis process within such groups. If an opportunity arose to compare the results across different industries the value would be enhanced still further.

1.6 SELECTING TECHNIQUES USING THE PRINCIPLES OF CREATIVE ANALYSIS

From what has gone before it will be inferred that there can be no definite system for selecting the best technique for any particular problem. The principles of creative analysis can, however, be used to suggest which general class of techniques may contribute to the solving and sometimes in which order.

The sort of reasoning behind a decision made on these lines is shown in Figure 1:11. The solver recognizes an open-ended situation with its concomitant need for creative thinking within the total process. If the problem could be clarified by an initial restructuring, then morphological analysis or one of these aids should be introduced. Once the problem is clarified, selection of individual or group techniques will be made in the light of the solver's sphere of influence. (In other words, he will start with individual techniques if he recognizes himself as the true agent.) Subsequent input of analytical or creative procedures will depend on the actual circumstances.

Figure 1:11 is an important illustration: through its assistance analysis of open-ended problems is made easier. Figure 1:11 is the basis of the examinations of the problems in Chapter 7 and can be applied to most of the case studies in Part Two.

Figure 1:10 Form for monitoring group problem-solving processes

1. Meeting date ____________ 2. Code ____________ 3. Client ____________

4 Problem title ____

5. Problem category ____________________________ 6. Organizer ____________

7. Composition of the group: names, background, familiarity with the problem (F_p) and with the techniques (Ft)

Name	Background	Fp	Ft	Name	Background	Fp	Ft

8. Pre-meeting observations ____

Figure 1:10 – continued

9. The meeting

9.1 Cooperation
9.2 Positivity
9.3 Acceptance of procedure
9.4 Level of speculation

9.5 Orientation time
9.6 Idea-generation time
9.7 Total ideas produced

9.8 Types of subroutines ______
SR(0) Pre-meeting orientation ______
SR(1) ______
SR(2) ______
SR(3) ______
SR(4) ______
SR(5) ______
10. Main objective(s) of the exercise ______

______

______

11. Post-meeting comments by participants

______

______

______

______

______

______

Figure 1:10 – continued

12. Meeting recorded by ______________________

13. Key individuals – idea development — names — Fp — Ft

14. Key individuals – evaluation — names — Fp — Ft

15. Evaluation procedures ______________________

16. Details of short-listed ideas ______________________

____

____

17. Approximate times for development and evaluation stages ______________________

18. Impact of exercise on client's actions
    (a) Within a month ______________________
    (b) After six months ______________________

19. Impact of meeting on his perception of the problem
    (a) Immediately ______________________
    (b) After one month ______________________
    (c) After six months ______________________

20. Summary of the exercise and how it might have been improved

Signed ______________________ Date ______________________

Figure 1:11 Decisions involved in the selection of suitable techniques for open-ended problem-solving

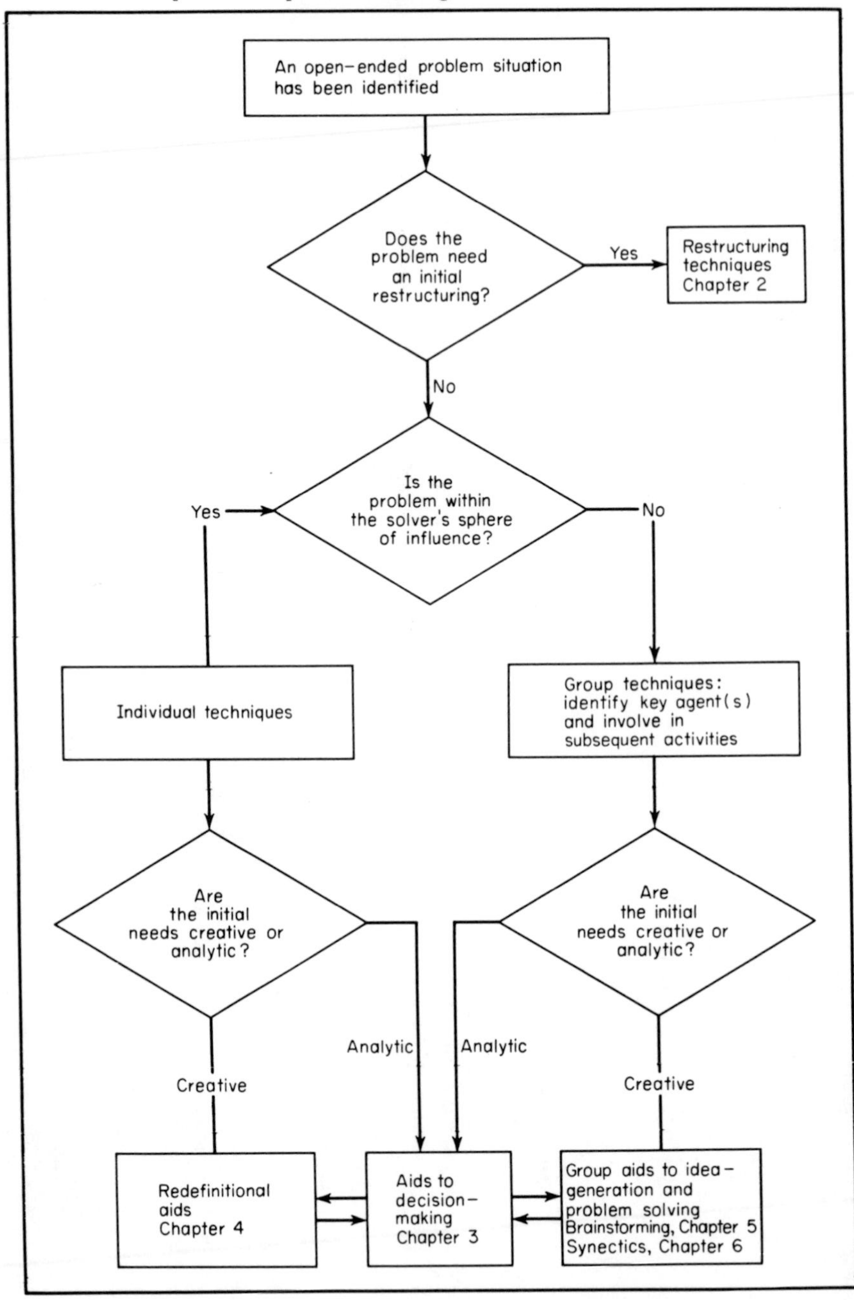

1.7 SUMMARY

There is a series of aids to solving open-ended problems. A solver can develop a flexible solving style by testing the aids or techniques on his own problems with a knowledge of the underlying principles (importance of the agent, creative and analytical techniques to be separate but interacting). He can then modify the elements (or subroutines) based on his own experience, in general following accepted principles, but being prepared to challenge any that conflict with his experimental observations. This process has been called creative analysis.

Chapter 2

Restructuring Techniques

2.1 INTRODUCTION

Managerial problems are often whole batteries of subproblems or activities. As well as having to overcome the individual difficulties, a manager needs a feel for the overall situation. People tend to do this by assembling a model or a simplified generalization which helps them to make specific judgements – for example, a research manager may have a model for innovation, in which he sees work done on basic research as having some impact on technical skills and eventual improvements to products; as he relates his model to specific experiences he can make his model more sophisticated and make valuable predictions from it. In general, managers could benefit from building simple models and the four restructuring techniques described here may help. (Those fortunate people who have specialist numerate skills may have experience in building far more complex structures for themselves. What follows is for the rest of us – a fairly large proportion of all managers, one might suspect.)

Problems which have to be restructured can be divided into those for which time and change are important considerations (dynamic) and those for which time and change are less important (static). (There will be situations which could fit both categories, and as a result there is considerable overlap in the use of techniques.) Typical uses and a distinguishing scheme are shown in Figure 2:1.

Figure 2:1 Distinguishing between uses of the different techniques for data structuring

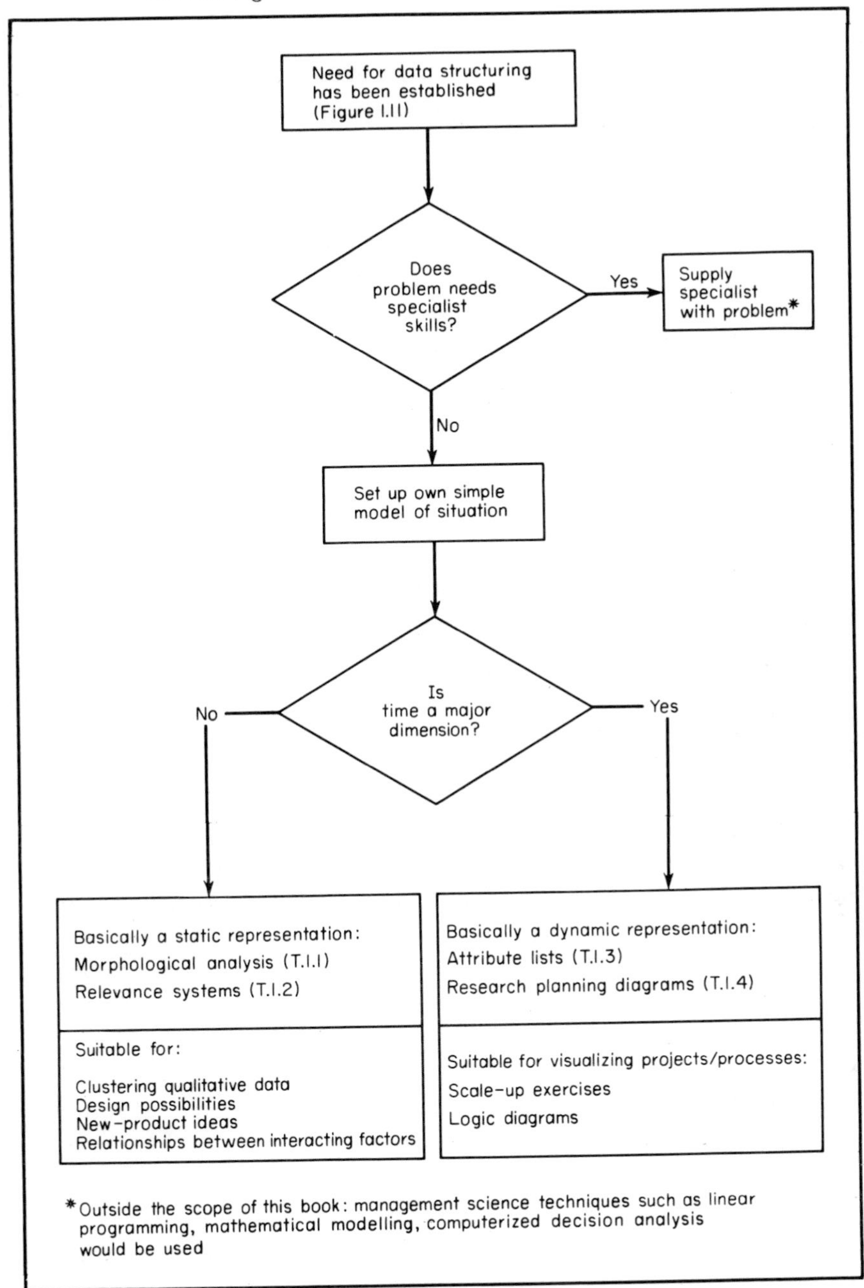

2.2 *MORPHOLOGICAL ANALYSIS (TECHNIQUE T.1.1)*

Complex problems often have to be represented simply and clearly so that there is less risk of the solver overlooking any aspects. Morphological analysis is an attempt to represent a problem in terms of its main aspects, which will be referred to here as *dimensions*. The simplest way of conducting a morphological analysis is an intuitive one, in which the analyst simply thinks of the two or three aspects of the problem which he considers to be critical and sets these up as the key dimensions.

Figure 2:2 illustrates a two-dimensional matrix which has been derived as an alternative representation of an agenda for a meeting of technical managers.

Several other representations could have been set up, for the matrix does not define the problem, it contains the problem (just as the x and y axes of a graph contain and do not define the functions represented). Different analysts will produce different representations according to their particular needs. The example in Figure 2:2 appears rather simple but there is evidence in every normal meeting that a single dimension does not cover all possibilities (the 'miscellaneous' item any other business). As the number of dimensions increases so the miscellaneous item is assimilated into the cells of the matrix.

Most textbook examples of morphological matrices are of a complexity that deters the average manager. Typically one finds new-product matrices with three or more dimensions and it has been known for members of a product development team to set up a matrix with many hundreds of individual cells, only to abandon it shortly afterwards in face of the work that would be involved in an exhaustive analysis. I have found the procedure more valuable for clustering together items within a set where the ordering is not initially clear – for example in a complicated report. Other clustering uses will occur to the manager according to his specific needs.

Matrices are convenient representations for diagrams – as shown in Figure 2:3. Matrices have also been used in technological forecasting and in project control. Typical dimensions might be (time; technical refinements; market applications) and (time; resources; projects). In each of these cases, the treatment of the problem is more as a static than a dynamic one, with the time dimension no more important than

Figure 2:2 *An agenda, part of which can be represented as a morphological matrix*

(*a*) Usual representation of the agenda

Minutes
1 Matters arising
2 Use of the gas/liquid chromatography (GLC) apparatus
3 Use of the infra-red spectrometry (IR) systems
4 Use of the ultra-violet spectrometry (UV) systems
5 Use of the atomic adsorption (AA) spectrometer
6 Any other business

(*b*) Two-dimensional representation of the idea-generation stages of the agenda

← Existing analytical services →

Uses	GLC	IR	UV	AA	Others
Faster service					
Modified/improved service					
Computerized results					
Upgrade operators					
Other suggestions					

Figure 2:3 A matrix for classifying business areas

Increasing technological novelty →

Increasing market novelty ↓

	No technological change	Improved technology Utilizing more fully the company's present scientific knowledge and production skills	New technology Acquiring scientific knowledge of production skills new to the company
No market change	Established products	Reformulation	Replacement
Strengthened market Exploiting more fully the existing markets for the company's present products	Remerchandizing	Improved products	Product-line extension
New market Increasing the number of types of consumers served by the company	New uses	Market extension	New business

(Shaded) Boundary of normal existing businesses

any of the others. In the really dynamic treatments, such as some planning diagrams (T.1.4) or flow charts, time is clearly a uniquely important dimension. Such matrices are the province of the specialist, and are often quantified and perhaps combined with a computer analysis.

The more sophisticated the matrix the more important it becomes to derive the dimensions rigorously. In these cases, the intuitive process may be replaced by a synthesis described by M. J. Allen, who uses matrices as methods for stimulating creative thought. The steps of

Figure 2:4 Steps in a systematic procedure for developing a morphological analysis

1. Break down the problem into smaller aspects, each written on a card
2. Leave the problem for a while giving your subconscious mind an opportunity to work on it (incubation period)
3. Return to the problem and add any extra ideas you may have on to additional cards
4. Examine the cards and build up groups of them which are related
5. Continue synthesizing the groups until a small number (no greater than 7) of important and distinct elements are obtained (dimensions)
6. Set out each dimension in a representation as in Figure 2:5
7. Examine the various combinations by moving the strips relative to one another

his procedure are shown in Figure 2:4. He recommends a maximum of seven dimensions, but any number above two presents some representational and manipulative difficulties. He suggests using a 'morphologizer' (Figure 2:5(*a*)) from which individual combinations of elements are visualized by moving one strip relative to the others. (Figure 2:5(*b*) shows an optional form, in which the dimensions are arranged concentrically, and are free to rotate relative to each other.)

2.3 *RELEVANCE SYSTEMS (TECHNIQUE T.1.2)*

Relevance systems help an analyst to assemble data in a way which shows interrelations between various subelements. One of the most common is the company structure chart, with the senior executives at the top and lines joining them to increasing numbers of people at different levels. This is essentially a pyramidal structure. In this case the situation is almost completely close-ended (inasmuch

Figure 2:5 Optional representation of a four-dimensional matrix

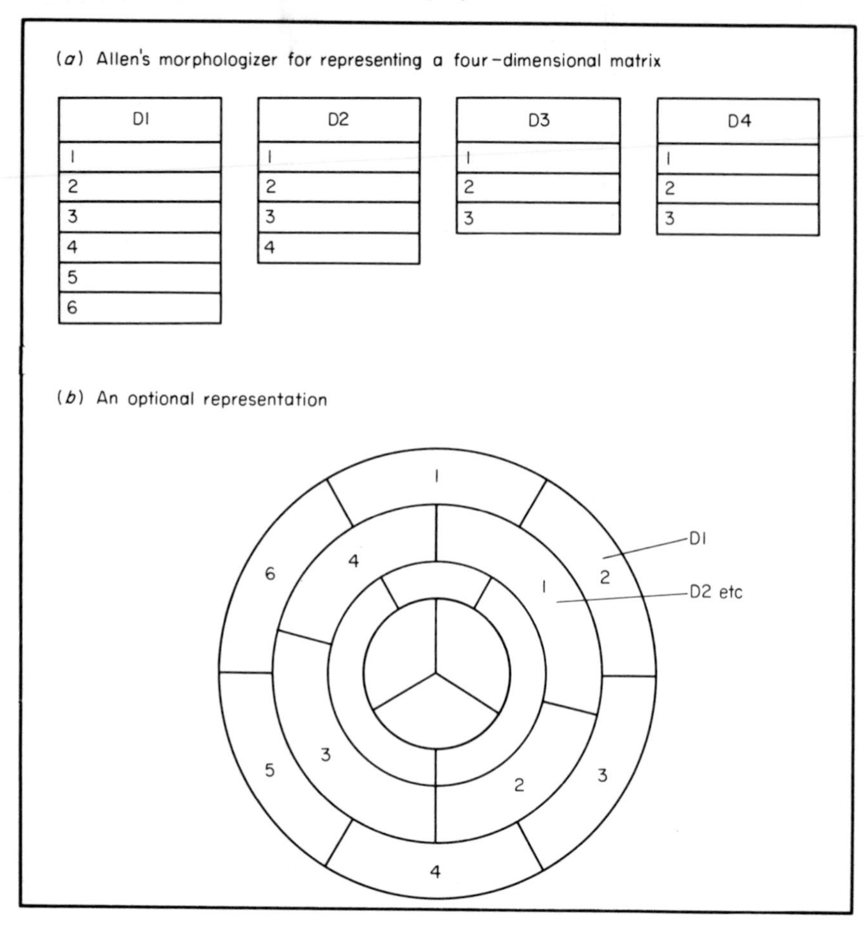

as the positions in the hierarchy are almost always accepted as true constraints and thus are not challenged). We will be more concerned with relevance systems in which the different items can be challenged and altered.

Two main systems will be discussed: single and binary relevance trees. A binary relevance tree is essentially two single relevance systems, displayed so that the interactions *between* as well as *within* systems can be examined.

An individual (single) system can be built up by one of two methods, rather similar to those available for morphological analysis. The first starts out with the postulation of highest-order elements, from which the lower-level elements can be derived sequentially moving down level by level. In the example of a company hierarchy, this would start by a postulated position for the chief executive. From this the numbers and types of managers reporting to him would be derived, and so on down the chart.

The second method is by building up towards the highest levels through a clustering process at lower levels. In practice the strength of the technique lies in operating both assembly processes, to challenge the validity of general concepts and objectives on one hand, and to enumerate relevant specific actions to obtain the objectives on the other.

Some examples will illustrate the scope of the technique. In recent years single relevance trees have been produced to describe the US space programme, the research plans for the UK Post Office, and objectives of government R and D programmes. A more day-to-day situation is represented in Figure 2:6 – a company's marketing strategy. For idea-spurring, the lower end of the relevance system should suggest specific actions – the elements should answer the question 'How?' (Combining the elements and examining at a higher level answers the question 'Why?') In practice some of the specific low-level actions overlap; in Figure 2:6, the objectives of increasing the mailing list *and* increasing visibility could be achieved by attending conferences. Overlaps give an increased weight to the actions involved.

The next step is to extend the technique to two interacting relevance systems. Suppose the marketing strategy of Figure 2:6 had to be integrated with the company's overall policy decisions. This is another relevance system, which could be related to the first as shown in Figure 2:7. The interface offers an opportunity for each system to influence the other. It permits the directors to re-examine the constraints implicit in their overall policy and the marketing staff to look at their plans in the context of overall company policy. For example, following up lost clients may conflict with the policy decision not to renew short-term contracts. A similar scheme was described in a recent article by Unilever corporate planner John Hubert (1970). His binary system was made up of company objectives and research projects and objectives. The system helps integrate R and D with the rest of the organization.

Figure 2:6 Relevance system for a company's marketing plans

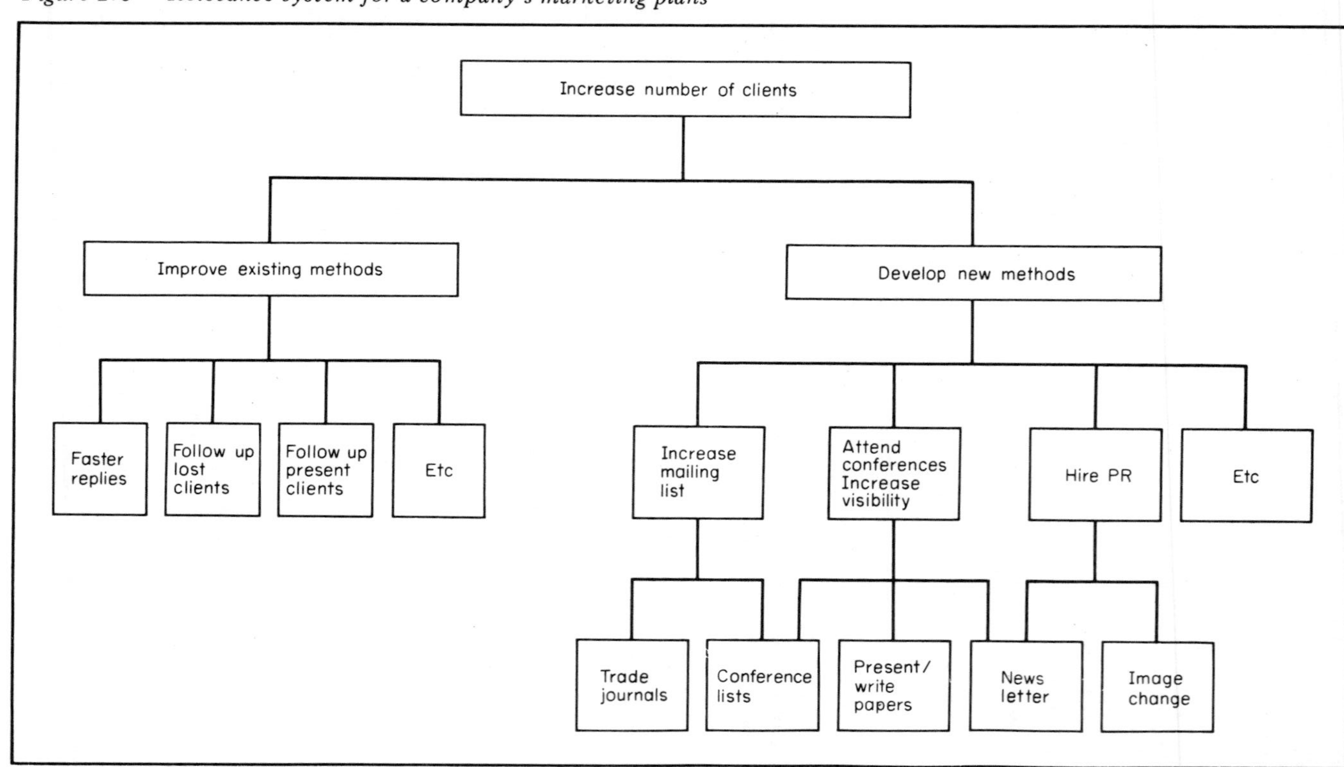

Figure 2:7 A binary relevance system

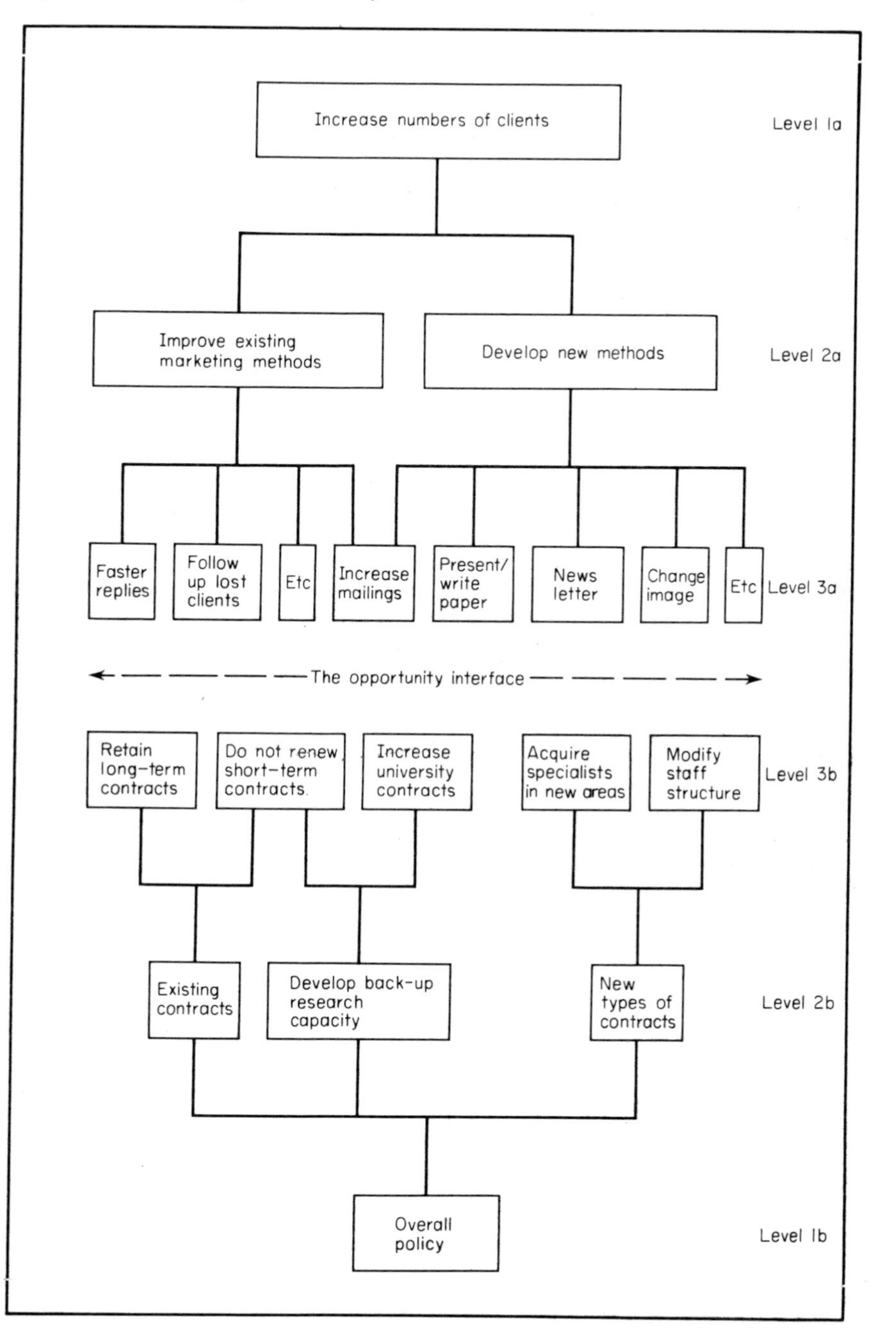

2.4 ATTRIBUTE LISTING (TECHNIQUE T.1.3)

Attribute listing is a specialized form of morphological analysis. The term is generally applied to an analysis of a product or process in terms of its functions or attributes (hence an alternative name functional analysis). Figures 2:8 and 2:9 illustrate the two main uses: representations of ideas for a product and a process respectively. The first is concerned with a system which can be considered independently of time or change (a static system) and the second is concerned with a system in which time and change become important and must be built into the analysis.

In either case morphological analysis should help the manager to separate concepts of functions from concepts of form. Thus, in considering new ideas for razors (Figure 2:8) attention is directed

Figure 2:8 *Attribute listing used in the representation of a static system.* A form of morphological matrix in which the functions or attributes make up the dimensions. In this case the implications of changes with time are not considered, and the system may be seen as essentially a static one.

Dimensions	*Elements within the Dimension*
Cutting surfaces	Steel blade, Steel strip, etc
Handle	Pen-holder, Integral with mounting, Cylindrical, Spherical, etc
Protective mounting for cutting surface	None, Spring-loaded, Push-button, Other
Cutting process	Manual slicing, Scissors action, Rotating horizontal, Rotating vertical
etc	etc

towards 'methods of removing hair' rather than towards blades and it becomes easier to anticipate new forms such as the rotating strip or the double blade.

Similarly, in the dynamic system of Figure 2:9, a drying system is considered in such terms as 'feed processes' rather than 'conveyor belts'. The analysis of dynamic systems is particularly important in engineering problems, where time and change are implied in the options within each dimension.

Figure 2:9 *Attribute listing used in the representation of a dynamic system.* Redrawn by permission of M. F. Woods and G. B. Davies (Unilever Ltd). First published by the Institution of Chemical Engineers, Symposium Series No. 35 (1972).

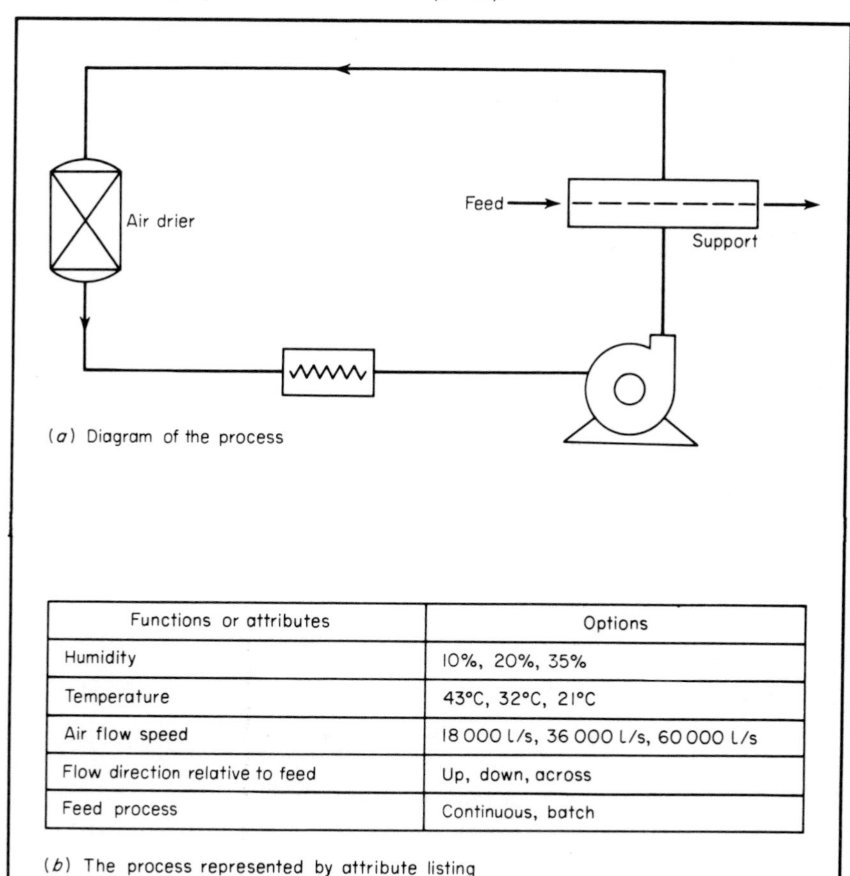

(*a*) Diagram of the process

Functions or attributes	Options
Humidity	10%, 20%, 35%
Temperature	43°C, 32°C, 21°C
Air flow speed	18 000 L/s, 36 000 L/s, 60 000 L/s
Flow direction relative to feed	Up, down, across
Feed process	Continuous, batch

(*b*) The process represented by attribute listing

It is important to distinguish between qualitative and quantitative variables, as attribute lists made up solely of quantitative variables may be tackled by mathematical techniques outside the scope of this book – including factorial analysis and random-walk optimizations.

In listing attributes it is probably helpful to remember that unless mathematical or computerized procedures have been adopted, there is a limit to the number of attributes that can be considered at any one time. The same rule of thumb applies as for morphological matrices – keep the number of dimensions to seven or less.

2.5 *RESEARCH PLANNING DIAGRAMS (TECHNIQUE T.1.4)*

Managers have been taught a whole series of procedures to help them plan their work and represent it in a meaningful way. Research planning diagrams seem to be a convenient compromise between the complexities of critical path networks or computer-aided methods, and the lack of detail of simple flow charts. The logic of the research planning diagram has been borrowed from computer flow diagrams, and follows these rules: actions are set in rectangular boxes; decisions are represented in diamonds; completion needs (actions which must be finished before another can begin) are indicated by ⊙ . In one technical laboratory the display is seen as a method whereby a project committee can examine a project proposal submitted to them. Setting up the diagram helps the proposer, by forcing him to consider possibilities of failure at critical points within the project. The advantages of this particular form of representation are considered to be that decision criteria have to be made explicit; the possibility of failure is also made explicit; and recycling (repeating a subroutine under varying conditions) can be clearly indicated. (This is not easy on some of the optional representations.)

The format of the research planning diagram is also suitable for programmed learning texts, and has been incorporated into many diagrams in this book. At the other end of the complexity scale, the format can be used with a computer simulation package to determine probabilities of success of a pathway as a function of cost or time. The computer can be programmed to print out the entire diagram. Figure 2:10 is redrawn from such a computer output.

Figure 2:10 *A research planning diagram identifying the activities within a process-modification exercise*

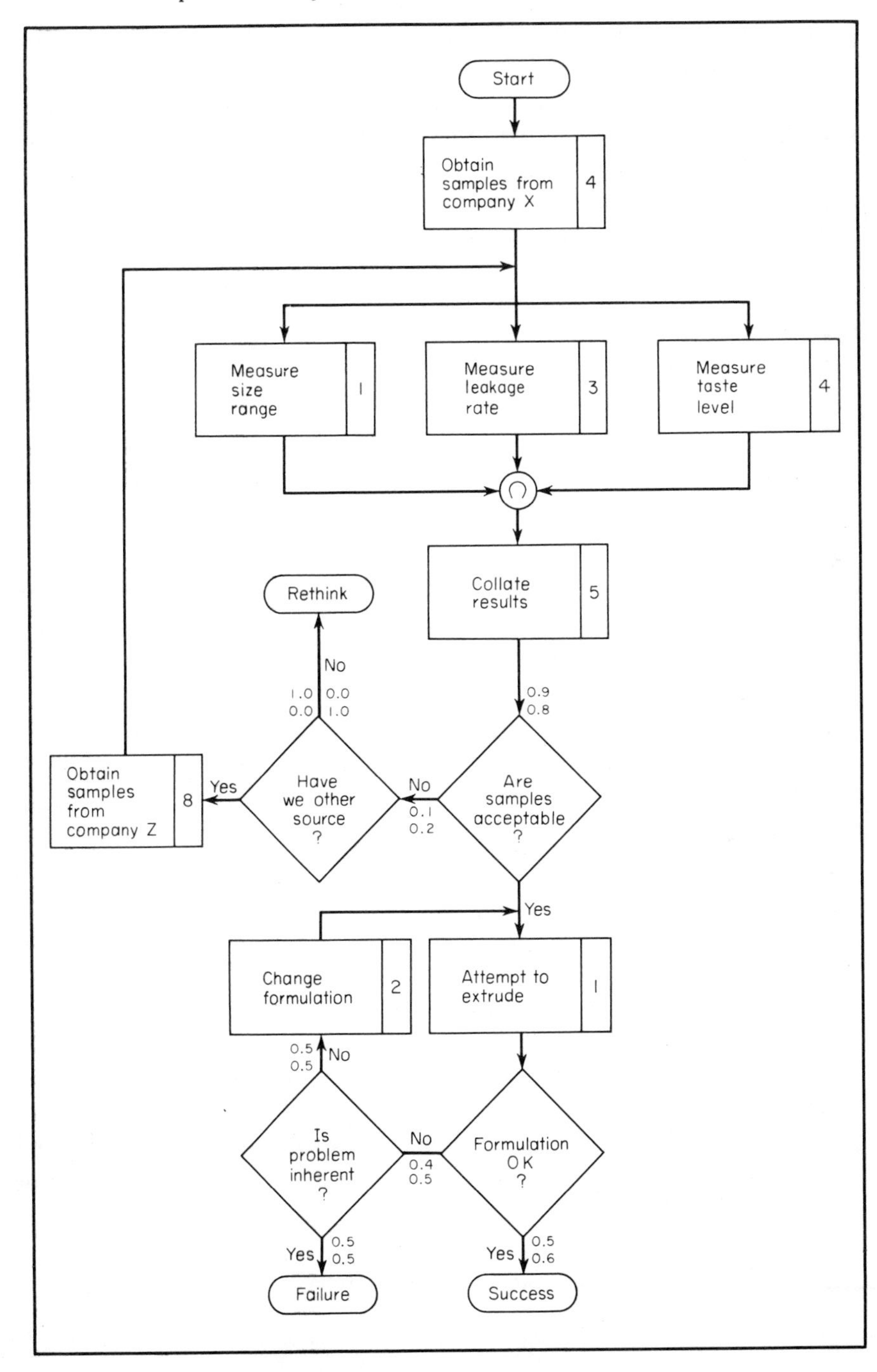

2.6 SUMMARY

Some problems are so complex they have to be represented clearly before idea generation or decision analysis becomes possible. Static situations can be represented by morphological analysis or relevance systems, dynamic ones by attribute lists or research planning diagrams.

Each of the representations can play an important part in solving open-ended problems by making objectives and constraints clearer and easier to recognize and challenge.

Chapter 3

Decision Aids

When a decision has to be made there is a tendency to believe the choice is more limited than is actually the case. ('We either stick the new factory *here* or in Newcastle'.) The open-ended approach is to accept that there is a whole series of options, according to the constraints that are being challenged ('Do we need a new factory? Can we have units here *and* in Newcastle?') But sooner or later decisions have to be made and situations accepted as effectively close-ended.

Therefore, it will be important to make sure that as many options as possible are being considered in the decision process. Once *all* the options have been established there are plenty of mathematical procedures for analysing them. This book will be concerned with two simple aids (checklists and weighting systems) which will help to set up a situation in which these more sophisticated techniques become valid. They can be used in a variety of decision-making contexts and provide a means for learning about basic assumptions and constraints.

In the overall scheme of problem-solving the decision aids are very much elements which become integrated with restructuring devices (Chapter 2), or serve to select and evaluate the best ideas from creativity-spurring aids which are discussed in Chapters 4, 5 and 6.

3.1 CHECKLISTS (TECHNIQUE T.2.1)

As expertise is built up about a subject, key elements will be identified. The expertise can be expressed as a list of items or checklist of these elements. The decision maker, by examining the list (his or someone else's) in a specific situation can make sure that he is not overlooking any important issues which might influence his decisions. (This is a rather grand way of describing how, intuitively, the housewife prepares a shopping list.)

Checklists are found in project-evaluation schemes, assessment of ideas for new products or processes and value-analysis exercises. The individual factors can be as few as a dozen or as great as 200, but in each case there are more factors than could be coped with manually and reduction into smaller numbers of more complex units (for example, by morphological analysis, T.1.1) provides information of a different type. Such reduction produces a matrix which provides information about the overall 'shape' or potentially important dimensions of a system and therefore the *potential* of ideas which might be generated within it, rather than the value of actual ideas which have been already produced.

Checklists can be set up using methods described in Chapter 5, and augmented with information found in the literature. A good example of a checklist of factors obtained in this way is shown in Figure 3:1. It was prepared to help managers consider how a project team should be assembled. Another version of a checklist, this time to help project evaluation, is shown in Figure 3:2. The developers took an earlier list and modified it to suit their needs. Similar lists can be prepared to help groups to identify new business opportunities. The lists can be sophisticated by employing weighting factors (T.2.1) or visualizations of the options to be considered, as in the product profiles (shown in part) in Figure 3:3. Here the checklist is used to build up a series of profiles over time of new products or business opportunities. Eventually the manager using them regularly will be able to recognize recurring patterns – for example, patterns of factors which are correlated. In the example shown in Figure 3:3, the profiles indicate that product 1 is likely to have a higher risk and a higher reward than product 2.

Figure 3:1 *Example of a checklist.*
Factors to consider when setting up a new-products group.

Objectives/posture
To look for opportunities
To identify constraints
To invent new products
To stimulate/catalyse
To play trouble-shooting/fire-fighting roles
To facilitate communications

Positioning in a company
As an OR group
Within the research department
Within the marketing function
As a separate autonomous unit within the company
As an autonomous unit contracted outside the company
As a corporate strategy group

Line of authority
Chief executive
Other board member
Divisional director (eg technical directors)

Personnel
Multi-disciplined
Include generalists
Include intelligent outsiders (secretary, inventor, consumer)
Different ages and status

Criteria of success
Profit
Attaining projected objectives
Develops managers
No criteria of success
Impact on organization
Patents
Publicity
Prestige impact

Financial position
Self-funding in long term
Shared funding with venture capitalists
Subsidized
Internal contracting
Carried as an overhead

Reward system for personnel
Bonus by results
Promotion back into company
Better involvement with own ideas
Independence
Security regardless of success of venture

Figure 3:2 Project evaluation checklist

Criterion	*Range*	*Rating*
Promise of success (P)	Unforeseeable	1
	Fair	2
	High	3
Time for completion (T)	Greater than 3 years	1
	1 to 3 years	2
	Less than 1 year	3
Cost of project (C)	Greater than £50 000	1
	£10 000–£50 000	2
	Less than £10 000	3
Need to company (N)	May fill a need	1
	Desirable	2
	Necessary now	3
Market gain (M) per year	Less than £400 000	1
	£400 000 to £1 million	2
	Greater than £1 million	3

3.2 WEIGHTING SYSTEMS (TECHNIQUE T.2.2)

Decisions can be quantified by estimating the relative values of the different options and by putting figures to the estimates. The process is best illustrated by an example. In Case Study 2 to be described later, a short-list of six new-product ideas had emerged as 'winners' from field tests with potential customers. The director of the project had to decide on the relative merits of the six in terms of his own criteria – market size, potential return on investment, technical feasibility and so on.

The criteria were developed in discussion by the project team, and a weighted score obtained for each concept (Figure 3:4). Favourable and unfavourable points were kept separate – because otherwise equivalent aggregate scores might be obtained from distinctly different types of products. (For example those with high risk and high reward would have similar scores to those with low risks but low rewards.) In this exercise the product with the highest favourable

Figure 3:3 *Product profiles used as a means of comparing the potential of product concepts.*
A complete profile would include marketing, R and D, financial and other factor categories. Each factor is assessed on a four-point scale: very good (4); satisfactory (3); unsatisfactory (2); very poor (1).

The shared area indicates the assessment of each factor, in some cases covering two of the four categories. Thus, product 1 is scored relatively neutrally on the first factor, relation to the existing markets (3 to 2), and product 2 is scored very highly (score of 4).

When such profiles have been built up for a variety of products and product ideas they will help the investigator recognize products with similar and dissimilar characteristics.

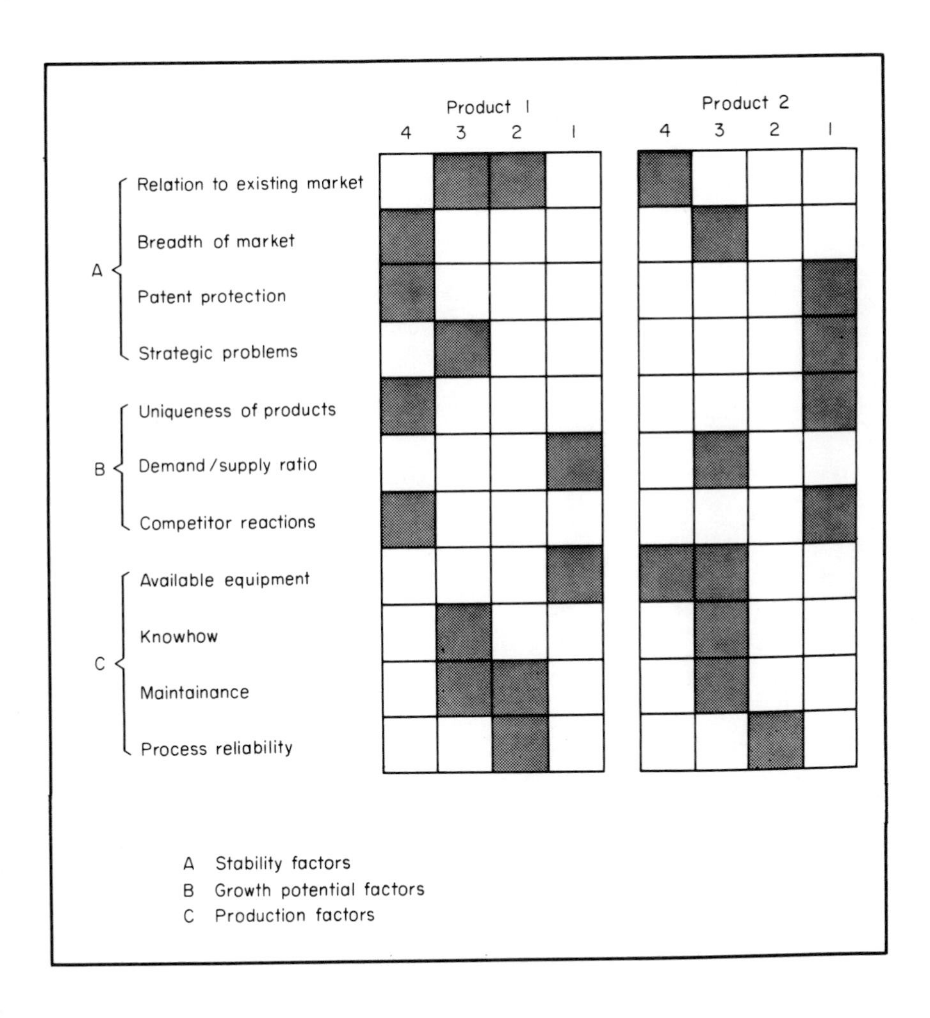

Figure 3:4 *Factor analysis used to evaluate the merits of six new-product concepts.*

A modified version of a weighting system used to evaluate the potential of six new-product ideas. (Various factors omitted for confidentiality reasons.)

STEP 1. Each new-product idea satisfied a list of 'musts' – criteria which had to be satisfied.

STEP 2. The potential value of each idea was calculated by summing the weighted scores assessed for a series of factors to contribute to the value.

STEP 3. The potential weaknesses or problems with each product were calculated in a similar fashion.

		New-product concept scores (*S*) and weighted score (*WS*)											
		1		2		3		4		5		6	
Factors	Weight (*W*)	*S*	*WS*	*S*	*WS*	*S*	*WS*	*S*	*WS*	*S*	*WS*	*S*	*WS*
Factors contributing to value													
Ease of establishing technical feasibility	9	6	54	7	63	2	18	3	27	5	45	8	72
Value of exclusivity	2	2	4	3	6	1	2	6	12	2	4	5	10
Potential sales	9	4	36	7	63	5	45	6	54	3	27	8	72
(Plus four other factors with weights from 8 to 2)													
Total weighted scores for potential value of each concept			144		233		176		220		164		275
Potential weaknesses													
Conflicts with existing products	6	4	24	2	12	2	12	2	12	4	24	4	24
Resource difficulties	9	5	45	2	18	5	45	5	45	3	27	2	18
(Plus three other factors with weights from 7 to 3)													
Total weighted scores for potential disadvantages			121		76		113		89		98		132

score had the highest unfavourable score as well, while the product with the next highest favourable score had a much lower unfavourable one.

It is important to realize that the analysis has *not* provided the answer to the problem 'which product should be progressed?' It has helped the analysts look on the problem in a systematic way and forced the team to consider such questions as 'Is a high return on investment more important than market size in the short term – in the long term?' and so on. As a result the team may indeed accept that the product with the best score is the one which should be progressed (it is assumed that resources are adequate for developing one new product at a time, in this study). But the team could equally find that a less-favoured product fits better into its plans for reasons which could never be built into a mathematical analysis. (Perhaps the team feels it would be more motivated to work on a technically interesting problem.) In this event the value in the analysis is that the team must be prepared to justify its actions all the more carefully if it proceeds on such a course of action.

As a result of such an analysis one can obtain a more penetrating understanding of the underlying principles of a complex situation and hence a basis on which to discuss assumptions and constraints. Senior managers may disagree with the judgement but in arguing the points in turn insights will be gained into the problem as seen at different levels in the organization.

3.3 MISCELLANEOUS INPUTS TO DECISION MAKING

Weighting systems operate best for evaluating a small number of options. When confronted with large numbers of possibilities some sort of clustering becomes necessary. Morphological analysis can reduce the options to a smaller number of more complex dimensions, which can then be weighted. For example, new product ideas could be clustered into new market areas. Once the most favoured areas have been identified by weighting procedures, additional ideas, focused more precisely to the specific areas, can be generated and evaluated by similar methods. (Another way of clustering ideas is represented in the screening system shown in Figure 3:5.) Such techniques become important after brainstorming exercises, when

Figure 3:5 Preliminary screening procedure for product ideas

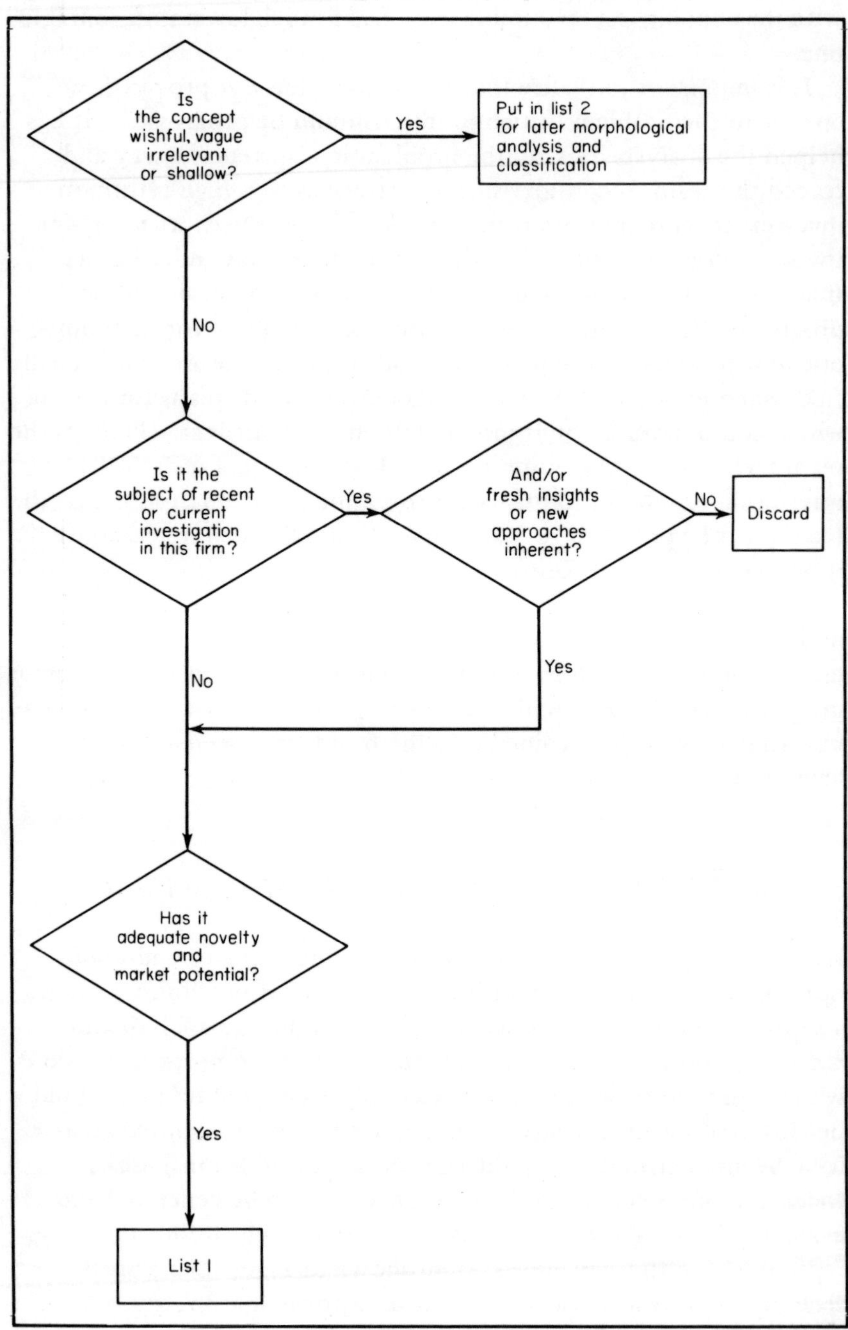

several hundred ideas may have been identified. Before leaving the topic of decision aids, it is worth considering one (often ignored) quality – intuition. Among professional managers, intuition is only acceptable in certain circumstances – for example by entrepreneurs, research scientists and venture managers. Yet many of our 'logical' decisions are based on intuitive assumptions, and such 'gut-feel' reactions are often accompanied by a high degree of motivation.

One of the arguments for letting research scientists follow their intuitive impulses is that in so doing they become motivated. If scientific discovery is partly dictated by chance, the overall probability of commercially viable discoveries should be higher if the scientists are motivated and thus producing a larger amount of output.

Provided 'gut feel' seems to be driving a worker in a direction which is reasonably acceptable to his manager, the argument holds in other fields. If three problem-solving ideas are suggested in a meeting and one seems to excite the person who has to implement the solutions, then the decision has to all intents and purposes been made. He will work on that problem first and devote most time to it. Attempts to influence him to the contrary may channel his motivation and creativity towards demonstrating why the other two ideas are not so good.

In this case, the point at issue is not the absolute value of the three ideas – from a practical point of view the winning idea is the one which gets worked on. In 'weighting-system' terms, it scores highly for the factor, 'level of acceptance by initiator'. Anyone not intending to implement the solution personally has to take that factor into account. The more open-ended the situation, the more will such human traits intrude on the decision-making process.

3.4 SUMMARY

In close-ended systems quantification of decisions becomes completely valid. To move towards decisions in open-ended problem situations it is important to obtain as many options as possible. Checklists and weighting systems help, but they should be seen as aids, not decision-makers in their own right.

In human situations intuition and motivation become important elements in decision-making. Provided 'gut feel' and logic point in the same direction the manager is fortunate. If they conflict, it is possible that the intuitive belief can suggest additional factors to be included in any 'logical' analysis of the situation.

Chapter 4

Redefinitional Procedures

4.1 TESTING YOUR REDEFINITIONAL STYLE

Before concepts are introduced which might alter your approach to problems in the short term, Figure 4:1 presents an opportunity to examine your own methods of problem definition and redefinition. It is far from being a scientific measure, but it does provide you with a chance for self-analysis which will help in guiding you through the rest of the chapter. Ideally you should work on the exercise with a break of hours or days between answering each of the three questions but this is not critical. If you cannot answer any of the parts of the exercise, note the fact, and return to it after finishing those parts which you could manage. When you have done as much as you can, use the results to find which techniques are most likely to help your problem definitional style, from Figure 4:2. Keep your results to compare them with another exercise, to be done after you have read this chapter.

4.2 PROBLEM SENSITIVITY AND REDEFINITION

The exercise may have demonstrated how unlikely it is in open-ended problems that the solver will hit on a satisfactory description at the outset. By definition the boundaries are fuzzy, and often the manager recognizes the more suitable definitions after he has started work on

Figure 4:1 An exercise to examine problem-solving style

1 Write down on a piece of paper an open-ended problem which is important to you and for which you would like some answers that could lead to action. Take as long or as short a time as you like to do this.

2 Again taking your own time, complete the following statements with reference to the open-ended problem you have chosen. If you cannot think of anything to write for a particular statement, move on to the next statement.

(*a*) 'There is usually more than one way of looking at problems. You could also define this one as . . .'

(*b*) '. . . but the main point of the problem is . . .'

(*c*) 'What I would really like to do is . . .'

(*d*) 'If I could break all laws of reality (physical, social, etc) I would try to solve it by . . .'

(*e*) 'The problem put in another way could be likened to . . .'

(*f*) 'Another, even stranger, way of looking at it might be . . .'

3 Now return to your original definition (1). Write down whether any of the redefinitions have helped you see the problem in a different way.

the problem. This gives the lie to the old belief that one must have the correct definition before initiating any problem-solving actions. In Figure 4:2 some common weaknesses in defining problems have been outlined. If it is possible to identify the most important needs in your personal circumstances, you will be able to concentrate on procedures developed to cope with these needs, which will be described later in this chapter.

The first common need is for definitional clarity. In a series of problem-solving seminars at Manchester Business School hundreds of problems have been supplied, from a large number of managers of different disciplines and levels of seniority. In a considerable proportion of the cases, the manager described at some length the overall situation without attempting to isolate any key issue. These cases illustrate the need for *clarity*. In discussing these problems, a group may suggest large numbers of new ways of looking at a situation, only for the person who made the original definition to insist that he had already defined the problem quite correctly and that redefinition was unnecessary. This attitude may be due to omniscience

Figure 4:2 Suggested techniques for improving problem-solving style

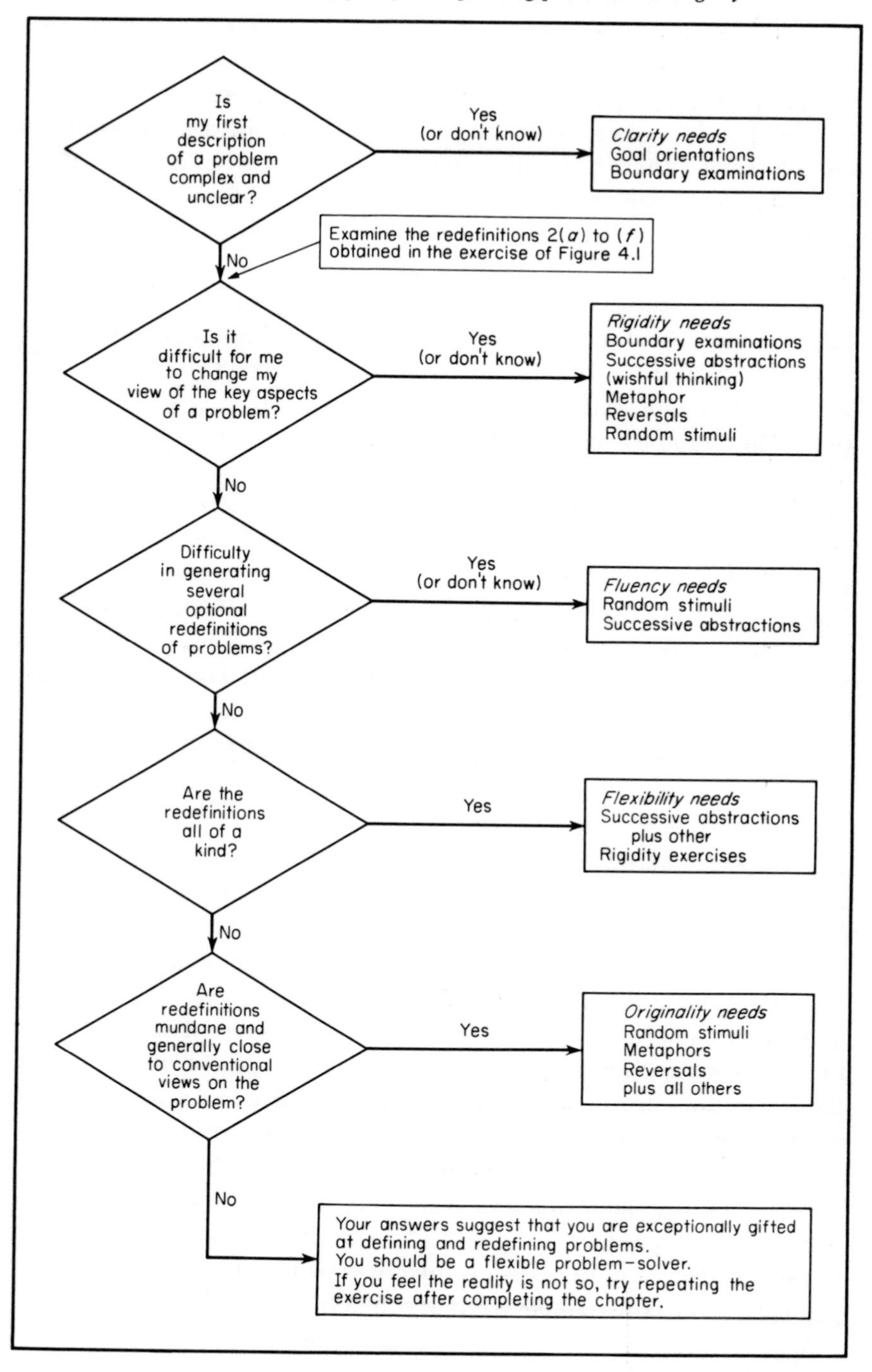

but I am more inclined to suspect *rigidity*. On occasions rigidity is broken down through good group interactions, and the solver accepts new insights and ideas.

The reverse of rigidity is the ability, unaided, to generate several options within a given situation (*fluency*). If the options are all of a kind, however, there is no improvement. The solver has a *flexibility* need. All these elements contribute to problem-solving style. In addition, there is a rare ability to produce redefinitions which are at the same time unusual yet meaningful (*originality*).

People who show redefinitional skills tend to produce original and valuable ideas. The techniques described in this chapter can be seen as starting points to obtaining such a problem-solving style. It has already been indicated that these techniques are of the 'water-wings' type. They can be used to bring about changes in your natural and intuitive problem-solving behaviour, which may not include the specific techniques in the long run. They can be practised in a clandestine fashion in conventional problem-solving meetings and particularly in the redefinitional stages of techniques such as brainstorming and synectics. You can also practise them when your mind has a chance to speculate (driving in to work, over coffee, when mowing the lawn). The state of mind is important. To be logical one has to concentrate on the problem; to obtain creative ideas one has to learn to relax and let the solutions come without effort.

4.3 GOAL ORIENTATION (TECHNIQUE T.3.1)

Goal orientation is first an attitude of mind and second a technique to encourage the attitude. Open-ended problems must be seen as situations where the boundaries are unclear but in which there may be fairly well-defined needs and obstacles to progress. There may also be areas which, after examination are accepted as close-ended (that is, the solver does not wish to challenge the boundaries around these areas). The close-ended parts are often called *constraints*.

The goal-oriented solver is constantly seeking to recognize *needs* ('what I want'), and *obstacles* ('what's stopping me getting what I want'). The technique is simply to adopt the habit (consciously at first) of asking 'What are the goals or objectives of the situation? What are the acceptable constraints? What are the obstacles?' Figure 4:3

Figure 4:3 Use of goal-orientation technique T.3.1

Original problem definition

We have a fork-lift truck which operates in a particularly hazardous environment. There is solvent vapour in the atmosphere; the flash-point is low and we are afraid there will be trouble from an explosion, or through the Factory Inspectorate.

Redefinitions:

1 (How to) eliminate fires in a potentially inflammable shed.

2 (How to) operate with existing fork-lift trucks (accepted constraint: keep existing trucks).

3 (How to) introduce new trucks at minimum cost (accepted constraint: cost of solution).

4 (How to) satisfy Factory Inspectorate of the safety of our newly adopted procedures.

illustrates the result from a training exercise using a real problem.

Goal orientation can demonstrate differences between problems whose definitions seem to place them in the same category and which are, therefore, likely to respond to the same approaches.

Consider the problems:

1 How to stop a bathroom tap dripping?
2 How to stop a motorway bridge leaking (after heavy rain)?

Semantically the statements are cousins. After redefining in terms of objectives however, the first is seen to refer to the objective of getting to sleep undisturbed; the second to reducing risks of erosion of the bridge or danger to motorists below.

4.4 SUCCESSIVE ABSTRACTIONS (TECHNIQUE T.3.2)

The principle of successive abstractions is akin to the relevance system (T.1.2). By varying the level of abstractions new definitional possibilities emerge. This is demonstrated in Figure 4:4. If the starting definition of a lawn-mower firm is 'to develop a new mower'— the higher level of abstraction gives 'to develop new grass-cutting

Figure 4:4 Successive abstraction technique T.3.2

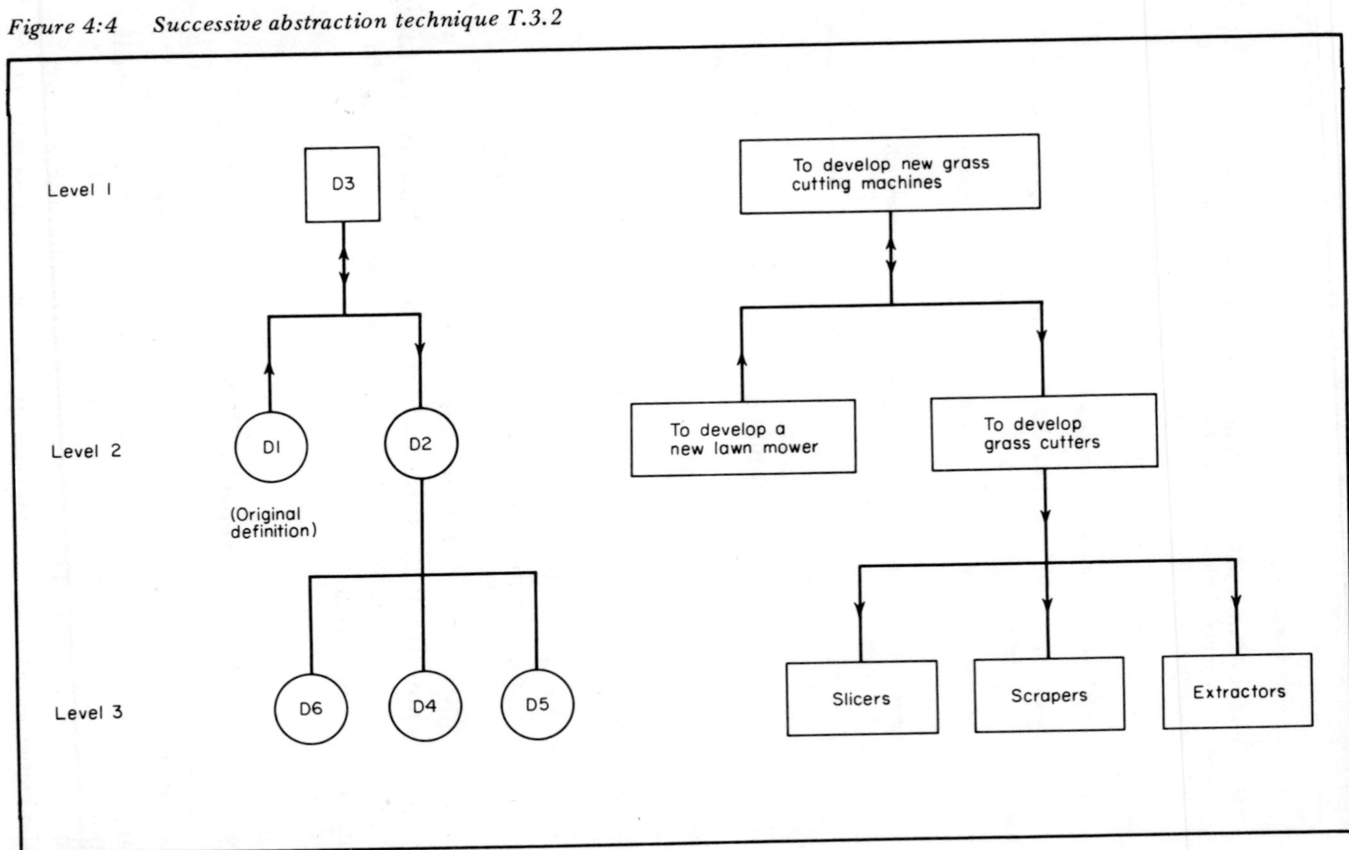

machines'. Returning to the lower level of abstraction gives a new appreciation of the market which the company is in. Descending to level 3 presents further possibilities. The extent to which the levels can differ from the original one will depend on the degree of open-endedness acceptable to the client. In this case, the manufacturer of grass-cutting machines might consider the higher-level abstraction for a market definition 'machines for cutting grass'. The manufacturer is unlikely to accept as useful the redefinitional level 'methods of stopping grass growing above a certain height' as this implies biological treatments likely to be outside the manufacturer's skills. The same problem examined by an agricultural institute might indeed be abstracted to such a level.

A manager with whom I once worked was particularly good at ascending the levels of abstraction. At times this was a good device, as he helped people see problems in broader terms. However, he also resisted attempts at getting down to specifics, saying that these were 'too convergent' a view of the problem. He was unwittingly being more obstructive of progress than the managers he accused of convergence. At least convergence to specifics makes some sort of action possible.

4.5 ANALOGY AND METAPHOR PROCEDURES (TECHNIQUE T.3.3)

Creative people often describe problems in terms of metaphor and analogy. Redefinitions in such nonliteral terms help increase one's chances of flexible problem redefinitions and creative solutions. In the group techniques (brainstorming and synectics) such redefinitions are highly acceptable to the leader, who will tend to prefer them to literal statements as starting points for further idea-generation activities. For example:

> 'How to improve the efficiency of a factory'
> is a down-to-earth statement,
> 'How to make the factory run as smoothly as an Appollo launch'
> is an analogical redefinition, and
> 'How to reduce organizational viscosity'
> is a metaphoric one.

The second and third statements are more productive of unusual ideas than the first.

Statements such as the first do not make it easy for the problem-solver to break away from his main previous lines of approach. In contrast, analogies and metaphors present whole new clusters of concepts which can be integrated into his thinking. In one example, the analogy of an Apollo launch might suggest methods related to countdown procedures to coordinate shift changeovers or to synchronize critical and complex operations. The second example, involving the metaphor of organizational viscosity can again spark off unexpected approaches – reducing poor interfacial operations between different groups by creating new communication responsibilities; deploying a manager who can stir things up at critical points in the concern; examining production lines for evidence of irregular flow patterns which might literally or metaphorically be streamlined.

4.6 WISHFUL THINKING (TECHNIQUE T.3.4)

Wishful thinking is not appreciated by many businessmen. They have to be precise, down to earth and logical. There is no time for fantasy. By adopting this attitude a rich source of new ideas is overlooked: through wishing for what might be, one can subsequently arrive at realistic and practical ideas which would not be easily derived without the transitional venture into fantasy. (Dr Edward de Bono in his works on lateral thinking describes an 'intermediate impossible' – a concept which can be used as a stepping stone between conventional thinking and realistic new insights. This is one example of wishful thinking.)

As with metaphoric redefinitions (T.3.3), a few wishful redefinitions can make a valuable contribution in formal problem-solving exercises. They are indeed closely related to metaphors and should not be treated too literally. For example, a food technologist is working on new methods of preparing artificial protein. In a moment of fantasy he considers his problem as 'how to build an artificial cow'. Although in practical terms this is wishful, the metaphor suggests that he should be looking at biological systems and perhaps at the means of converting cellulose into protein known to work in nature.

In practice it seems that some people can easily produce wishful redefinitions while others are more able to see the practical implications and return to earth with good ideas. In a group situation both provider and accepter can be present. When thinking on one's own, however, one has to do both. I have found the following device suitable. When I am worried that my thinking on some problem is repeating the same old things like a jammed record player, I try to complete some sentence such as:

> What I would *really* like to do is . . . or
> If I could break all the constraints I would . . .

This device sets up the new thinking pattern. The next phase is to return to reality. If possible there should be several steps rather than a sudden return. Again there are uncompleted sentences which help the process (in my case):

> . . . but as I can't really do that [for example make an artificial cow] what I could do is . . . [for example see which elements of mammalian protein synthesis I can repeat in the laboratory]. And in practical terms that means . . .

Examples of wishful thinking can be found in the case studies of individual problem-solving in Part Two, where the intuitive production of wishful ideas often plays an important part in the development of creative ideas.

4.7 NONLOGICAL STIMULI (TECHNIQUE T.3.5)

The power of introducing an unexpected element into a problem situation can be seen in several different environments. A fresh stimulus jerks the mind out of its set of assumptions. The Delphic order of forecasters, for example, kept careful and precise records of natural events but more often than not predictions were sparked off by examination of (presumably) unrelated objects. A long line of forecasters, soothsayers, gurus and so on have gazed at entrails, crystal balls, patterns in the dust, tea leaves and palms. The stimulus received gave them new insights. In the last century many people believed that any problem could be solved by opening the Bible at random and selecting a verse. This would indicate the solution. The little red book of *Quotations from Chairman Mao* is similarly invoked in China today. This may appear superstitious and old fashioned but one should remember the common phenomenon often described by modern managers as the opposite page effect. A manager goes to the library to follow up a reference. He finds the article on the opposite page will give him a lot more ideas.

It seems likely that if a person is motivated to solve a problem then he constantly scans for new approaches but at the same time fails to see any inputs which challenge his perception of the overall problem. Then, when his guard is down, some particularly unexpected element slips past his protection and he sees its relevance. In solving a problem by introducing fresh ideas the solver often makes relationships between concepts which have no logical connection. A facility to do this is a sign of a flexible and original thinker. If the solver is exposed only to stimuli which have generally recognized associations with his problem, these unusual connections are less likely. It can therefore be argued that there is value in exposing the problem-solver to a variety of apparently irrelevant experiences. In practice one of the most powerful stimuli is discussions with other people, preferably with less experience of the problem than the solver. One European company (Case Study 9) introduced out-of-focus slides (visual stimuli) and a series of sounds to help generate new ideas. Dictionaries have also been recommended.

As an exercise the reader may try the procedures outlined in Figure 4:5. In many instances the technique does not redefine the problem directly, it merely points the way to including elements which had previously not been associated with it.

4.8 BOUNDARY EXAMINATIONS (TECHNIQUE T.3.6)

When one defines a problem one makes a statement about its boundaries as one sees them. Provided one accepts that these are open to modification, the definition is only a starting point to problem-solving. Unfortunately people do tend to treat definitions as immutable. One way of helping to demonstrate that they can be changed is to take a statement regarding the boundaries and examine it phrase by phrase for the hidden assumptions. The following is a hypothetical example:

Figure 4:5 An exercise in nonlogical stimuli

For this exercise you will need pencil and paper and a pocket dictionary or book index.

1 Write down as many uses as you can think of for a piece of chalk.

2 When you can think of no more ideas let your eyes wander to some object in your range of vision with no immediate connection with the piece of chalk.

3 Try to develop new ideas stimulated by the object.

4 Now repeat stages (2) and (3) with a second randomly selected object.

5 Open the dictionary and jot down the first three nouns or verbs you see.

6 Try to develop new ideas stimulated by the words in turn.

7 Examine your ideas produced with and without stimuli for differences in variety (flexibility) and total numbers (fluency).

> Problem statement: How to develop the motorway network to allow for gradual replacement of rail by road transport as a consequence of relative lack of flexibility of the former.

The underlined words can all be debated. Should the motorway network be developed or could existing trunk roads be improved? Will replacement of rail be gradual or sudden? Will rail be the only consideration – what about airfreight? Is rail relatively inflexible – consider the Channel tunnel. And so on. The analysis may produce a 'better' problem definition. It is more likely to make the solver aware of the blurred nature of problem boundaries and the importance of a flexible open-ended problem-solving approach. The procedure is particularly suited for coping with management teams who are excessively precise in their attitudes towards project briefs and definitions.

4.9 *REVERSALS (TECHNIQUE T.3.7)*

Sometimes the best way to do something is not to do it. This means that by turning a problem on its head and examining the paradox one can see new approaches. In advertising this is a well-known trick. If a product has a weakness, it might be possible to hide the weakness.

Turn the problem on its head and then search for ways of publicizing the weakness. Thus foods of low nutritive value are hailed as supreme for the diet conscious; furniture which will not last becomes disposable; artificial becomes scientifically synthesized, and so on.

Responsiveness to reversals is a good measure of an individual's redefinitional flexibility. A manager who recognizes a valid weakness in his stated position can either reject the position entirely, or use it as a starting point for more valuable insights by an attitude of 'Well, in that case let's turn it on its head and see how . . .'

4.10 AN EXERCISE TO PRACTISE THE USE OF THE REDEFINITIONAL AIDS

At the beginning of the chapter in Section 4.1 you were invited to define one of your own problems, unprompted, and then helped by prompting sentences. You should now repeat the exercise using each of the seven redefinitional aids T.3.1 to T.3.7. As well as giving you a better idea of the aids you may see which have helped in your particular case, working once again from Figure 4:2.

If you try this exercise beware of the natural tendency to appreciate and enjoy using those techniques at which you are already skilled. The naturally flexible and fluent thinker may already be satisfactory at producing unusual responses and should concentrate on disciplining methods (such as boundary examinations, or the structuring techniques of Chapter 2).

4.11 SUMMARY

Redefinition is the key to open-ended problem-solving. Definitions should be accepted as starting points which change as experience of the situation is gained. Techniques exist to introduce flexibility into a solver's attitudes towards problems. These have to be used consciously but with practice the principles can be assimilated into an intuitive part of one's behaviour. The practice is best executed in an informal fashion by playing around with the problems, in as relaxed a way as possible.

Chapter 5

Group Techniques based on Brainstorming Principles and Practice

5.1 *INTRODUCTION*

Recently in the popular television series 'Softly Softly', police chief John Watt assembled his staff for a briefing: 'We are now', he announced 'about to have what the bright boys and management consultants call a brainstorming'. This example might be taken as typical of the use of the term to mean any sort of general discussion to turn up new ideas.

We will see that there is a quite precise use of the term as a method of group idea-generation and much of the criticism of the technique is based on the beliefs of people (like John Watt) who use the term in a more general manner. Brainstorming was developed as a method of generating ideas by an advertising executive, Alex Osborn, in the late 1930s. He described his methods in an important and definitive book called *Applied Imagination* in which he quoted the following dictionary definition of the verb brainstorm:

> to practise a conference technique by which a group attempts to find a solution for a specific problem by amassing all the ideas spontaneously contributed by its members.

He emphasized that no conference can be called a brainstorming session unless specific rules are included which require that the idea-generation stages be separated from the evaluation stages. (Individual brainstorming is known and is discussed in Osborn's book. In practical terms however, it can be considered as an optional procedure for the redefinitional techniques of Chapter 4 and is not considered here.) It is often assumed, from incorrect interpretation of Osborn's intentions, that during a brainstorming session there is no control over emotions or the direction in which the meeting proceeds. One might therefore conclude that such a technique is illogical, and the practitioners lacking in judgement. A famous criticism made in *Fortune* magazine some years ago described it as 'cerebral popcorn'. It is quite correct that during the idea-generation stage no evaluation is permitted. But judgement is postponed, not abandoned, and in the subsequent analytical stages evolution of ideas is at least as rigorous as in a conventional meeting. By 'postponing' judgement, I mean relaxing and letting ideas come; the first stage towards achieving this is to make a determined, conscious effort to refrain from evaluation.

Osborn's earliest brainstorming concentrated on commercial and educational problems. Later the technique was to be tested, and modifications developed in a variety of circumstances on problems of a technical, military, financial and aesthetic nature by groups throughout the world. In Holland a rent-a-brainstorming service exists with part-time participants from all walks of life. In Denmark, one successful inventor and industrial magnate encourages his staff to have at least one brainstorming session for new-product ideas every week, as he believes that practising the technique increases an inventor's capacity to produce a regular stream of original ideas. In West Germany when a well-known market research agency recently assisted a major consumer goods firm in a diversification exercise, at least three new products were marketed which owed something in their development to brainstorming exercises. Management seminars in Belgium and Italy have discussed the technique and given case studies. In the UK one senior management consultant, Geoffrey Rawlinson, has given demonstrations of brainstorming to literally hundreds of managers over the last decade. Examples of successes emerging from brainstorming sessions will be found in the case studies of Part Two.

There are hundreds of references to brainstorming in the literature.

Unfortunately these deal almost exclusively with the process as described by Osborn. Furthermore, a large proportion come from carefully controlled experiments conducted on contrived problems and with artificially composed groups such as students. These exercises show that Osborn's principle of postponement of judgement is justified in practice. The rest of this chapter will look at less publicized but equally important aspects of the original (Osborn), technique and more modern variations of it.

5.2 SUITABLE TOPICS FOR BRAINSTORMING

In the overall scheme of open-ended problem-solving (Figure 1:11), brainstorming is suggested along with synectics as the preferred technique for situations which require creative group insights. If the problem is particularly complex it would first be restructured and only then tackled by brainstorming or synectics.

Some help in deciding which technique to adopt can be obtained through considering the importance of the client; the need for creative insights and the sort of output that is wanted. My own preference is for brainstorming when the presence of an expert is not likely to be critical for a successful idea to be produced, when a high level of creativity is a bonus rather than a necessity and when the output is needed as a quantity of ideas derived rapidly from a heterogeneous group of people. These factors are summarized in Figure 5:1. In practice the decision tends to be tackled intuitively and for a significant proportion of problems no clear preference can be established. In these cases both methods could be tried. Figure 5:2 lists problems which have been brainstormed satisfactorily in recent exercises.

To reinforce the point further, Figure 5:3 lists problems and types which have been brainstormed, but which, for various reasons, proved less suited to the technique.

5.3 SELECTING A BRAINSTORMING GROUP

Having established that a problem is to be tackled in a brainstorming session the next step is to select a group of people. For this, group size and types of participants both have to be decided. In practice the

Figure 5:1 *Factors favouring brainstorming rather than synectics as an idea-generation technique.*
The problems should have been previously categorized as suited for a group problem-solving technique using Figure 1:11. The factors listed in this figure help the solver select brainstorming or synectics as the preferred technique.

	Factors favouring brainstorming	*Factors favouring synectics*
Presence of the client	Not a key factor for production of ideas (but to be recommended from motivational considerations)	Ideas not likely to be produced as easily in the absence of a client (regardless of motivational considerations)
Significance of new insights	Usually a bonus but may not be necessary	Solutions may require a high level of new insights
Output from a problem-solving session	Simple 'crystallized' concepts in large quantity needed quickly and covering as many aspects of the problem situation as possible	Smaller numbers of concepts developed in some detail and complexity often requiring subsequent tests before their value can be established

size of the group is often only partly under the control of the organizer who will have to work within the constraints. Osborn recommended a group of approximately ten people, half of whom were experienced 'core' participants. The group was conducted by two leaders.

My own preference for Osborn-type brainstorming is for a smaller group made up largely from a pool of contributors who have taken part in a few brainstorming and synectics sessions and have been generally positive and productive. Six or seven such people will produce ideas at a rate which is about as fast as can be comfortably recorded. Increasing the group size can have a negative effect if it becomes difficult for the individual members to get their ideas recorded rapidly. As well as forgetting ideas, the members become frustrated, and have time to evaluate their own ideas, thus getting away from the principle of postponement of judgement.

Figure 5:2 Problems suited to brainstorming exercises

Problem types	*Specific reasons for suitability*	*Examples*
New concepts for products New concepts for markets	Large number of ideas needed from different people with different experiences	New uses for glass New markets for a commercial patent New food concepts for consumer testing
Trouble shooting and planning	Need for a rapid collection of views Need to identify as many significant factors as possible	Anticipating problems during a scale-up project Reducing factory-chimney emissions Identifying divisional or company future needs
Managerial problems	Problem often requires production of a cross-section of views without undue inhibition by status	Improving safety performance Reducing warehouse losses Tangible rewards for outstanding work performance
Process improvements	Suggestions are additive	Value-analysis exercise (various) How to meter bulk materials better How to maintain a cold-room more cheaply

Figure 5:3 *Problems not suited to brainstorming exercises*

Problem types	*Specific reasons for unsuitability*	*Examples*
Problems with one or a small number of correct answers; problems which appear to have only one sort of answer	Problem is not sufficiently open-ended Analytical thinking preferred	Who should be in charge of the company's diversification? Which chemicals should we try next to produce the desired effect?
Extremely diffuse and complex problems	Initial sessions produce a wide range of vague solutions which essentially redefine the problem. Restructuring becomes necessary, might have been better before brainstorming	What should the company do to save money? How to reduce global pollution
Problems where the main obstacle to solution is the decision-making process	Analytical type of thinking preferred	Where should we relocate our research laboratories?
Problems demanding an extremely high level of specific technical expertise (eg mathematical or organic chemical problems) which seems to necessitate a group with rather homogeneous background experiences, or simply individual activity	Heterogeneous groups are preferred for brainstorming	How to synthesize compound X by a novel patentable approach
Problems requiring the manipulation or motivation of people who can never be involved in the exercise; problems without a client fully committed to the brainstorming	Incorrect evaluation of the spheres of influence of the participants	How to persuade the company board to give my group more money

On the other hand, a larger group is often convenient for introducing trigger sessions, or when the general level of brainstorming experience is low (which reduces the speed of idea production).

The group should represent as many disciplines as possible who will be able to understand the problem and contribute to it. The members should not, however, be selected for expertise in the problem – on the contrary they should be disinterested but capable of contributing. For technical problems some level of scientific training might be desirable but no more than one would expect an intelligent person to have picked up through 'O' level studies and association with managers in technology-oriented projects. For problems which relate to the 'average customer' the group will almost certainly benefit if such semi-mythical creatures are available. Secretaries are often particularly good and display fewer inhibitions than some junior managers when included in a group with senior personnel.

The perceived creativity of the members is less critical than their abilities to work constructively in meetings. Selection should be on a trial basis for training purposes, excluding those people unhappy with the technique in later exercises. Operating on a volunteer basis helps – the unsympathetic person is unlikely to want to be involved in more than one exercise.

The criteria for selecting a group are summarized in Figure 5:4.

5.4 OSBORN-TYPE BRAINSTORMING (TECHNIQUE T.4.1)

The form of brainstorming originated by Osborn is still the most frequently adopted variation. The total problem-solving system comprises a pre-meeting preparation to establish that the problem is suitable, a warm-up session to start the meeting and the actual brainstorming. As with other variants, the meeting is just the starting point to the real work of reporting, evaluating and progressing the ideas.

Preparation

The level of preparation will be partly settled by circumstances and will be partly under the control of the organizer. He should spend some time with the client digesting and defining the problem together. If time permits a résumé of the discussion should go to the group, asking

Figure 5:4 Criteria for selecting brainstorming groups

Experience	Include at least two people who have taken part in half a dozen sessions, if possible, and at least two to whom brainstorming is a new experience
Background disciplines	For new insights seek a wide spread of backgrounds but dictated by the problem
Personality of the candidates	The candidates should have shown good and constructive attitudes in normal meetings. This is more important than individual creativity which each candidate is believed to possess
Company seniority	A wide range of seniorities is desirable if the group can work together but may make the leader's task more difficult. (It will also increase chances of new insights and later progression of ideas)
Inclusion of the expert(s)	The putative expert or agent (responsible for progressing the ideas) should be included. No group should have two members who might see themselves as equally competent to act as expert
Group size	Five or six people, recorded round robin (T.4.3); six to eight, Osborn (classical) (T.4.1), the larger size being suited to less experienced groups; larger can be handled in trigger sessions (T.4.2) (up to about 15 people), but still larger groups should be split into subgroups

them to consider new ways of looking at the problem and to bring any ideas along with them to the meeting. (In practice the motivation of brainstorming groups to solve the problem is initially quite low – I have never heard of a group member approaching a client before a meeting with a solution to his problem. This may be no bad thing, as if people do think about the problem during this period, it will be in a relaxed and disinterested fashion, often a good attitude for producing original ideas.)

Warm-up session

The total time available for brainstorming should be organized so as to permit at least an hour and a half warm-up, leading up to the actual idea-generation. A period of problem redefinition can be included at the end of the warm-up (for about 15 minutes if necessary).

Some problems are more easily redefined during the meeting; others will be adequately defined before it, during the preparation session.

The purpose of the warm-up is to take a set of individuals, with personal prejudices and vested interests, and help move them into a temporary state in which they all work together and in which ideas are accepted and developed without evaluation. At the start of any meeting people tend to sit rather rigidly and arrange their positions according to disposition and 'pecking order'. A formal table and hard chairs will remind people of conventional work meetings; a semicircle of easy chairs, with low tables for ashtrays and writing materials will help produce a more relaxed mood. The methods which might be adopted to relax a group are endless and a serious practitioner could well study the principles and practice of encounter groups (see Case Study 9 for examples of these). Other procedures, enumerated in Figure 5:5, have been found satisfactory with a wide variety of groups of managers of varying degrees of experience and sophistication in brainstorming.

Figure 5:5 *Procedure for a warm-up session before a brainstorming.* Recommended minimum warm-up period is an hour and a half.

Exercise	*Notes*
Group discussion (5–20 minutes)	Improving creativity in this organization. (Short presentation followed by discussion.)
Creativity tests (5 minutes each) total 30 minutes	Test your flexibility, fluency and originality. 'Uses of a piece of cheese'; future scenarios; improving a child's toy; creative doodling. (5 minutes plus discussion.)
Redefinitional exercises (10–20 minutes)	T.3.1 to T.3.7
Practice brainstorming (10–20 minutes)	A dry run – rules explained, exercises similar to the creativity tests and redefinitions. Examples of good brainstorming procedure discussed
Redefinition of the problem (10–15 minutes)	Optional
'Building' exercise (0–5 minutes)	If there is insufficient 'building' (improving on ideas) during exercises 3–5, this exercise helps each member in turn to practise extending ideas on redefinitions already produced

There is a temptation to reduce the warm-up time for experienced groups. This should be avoided, as the procedures help the members to escape from the pressures and prejudices imposed on them through their everyday actions. These cannot be cast off at will, regardless of the experience of the members in brainstorming. In weekend intensive workshops it seems to take several sessions for a group to work together confidently and for all these reasons, the warm-up should be conducted for at least an hour and a half with an experienced group.

Idea-generation procedures

At some stage of the warm-up procedure the leader explains how the group will be expected to behave while generating ideas. It is becoming less necessary, with increasing sophistication among managers, to labour this point but a summary of the main principles could be written up and left conspicuously in front of the group, as in Figure 5:6. Key redefinitions will have been identified earlier (in the pre-meeting with the client, or during the warm-up redefinitional stages). These will be in open-minded format (a 'how to . . .' statement is a convenient way to convert more verbose problem statements into a suitable form). The group then attempts to produce ideas at speed to satisfy the redefinition. The essentials of each idea should be captured – the most convenient way being to write all the ideas on a flipchart. Details are given in Case Study 14. Shorthand-typists and tape-recorders have been advocated but such refinements make the whole technique less flexible.

Figure 5:6 *Principles of 'Osborn-type' brainstorming as they might be explained and written up in view of the group.*
The leader explains the rationale behind the principles in his own words. American version is 'Postpone judgement, freewheel, hitchhike, quantity breeds quality'.

Try to relax and let the ideas come to you of their own accord

Don't evaluate ideas at this stage

Listen and improve on other people's ideas

The more ideas produced – the more good ideas will be present

As mentioned earlier, the speed of idea production should be used as a measure of the group's postponement of judgement. When ideas are verbose, and contain justifications and qualifications, the meeting is close to a conventional one.

A group of six to eight people brainstorming correctly should produce ideas at a rate which is just comfortable for the leader to note all the statements on the flipchart (about five or six a minute). Each page of the chart then provides stimuli for fresh thoughts.

Ideas flow freely at first from a group that has warmed up adequately and is dealing with a suitable problem. However, the initial ideas tend to be individual efforts which ignore the potential stimuli of the other ideas being produced. As a result there may be a slump as the members of the group begin to exhaust their supply of ideas. The leader should let the session proceed beyond this slump (during which time there are rather long pauses in between the production of ideas). Once past this difficult period the members rediscover the value of stimuli from other people's ideas and produce more and more original combinations of ideas. There is some evidence that the best ideas occur at that time.

For extremely open-ended problems the slump is less noticeable and the ideas all much the same. In either case groups tend to become excessively frivolous or bored after about half an hour and a change of procedure is recommended. At this stage the meeting should be particularly relaxed and evaluation should be postponed until the other idea-generation variations have been worked through.

During the meeting the leader can introduce his own ideas to keep up the flow and speed. I prefer to ask open-ended questions, although it may be even better to tolerate silence (particularly mid-session) as this creates a special sort of tension which is released in a further flow of ideas.

5.5 TRIGGER SESSIONS (TECHNIQUE T.4.2)

A trigger session is a group idea-generation process in which members work independently for a period producing a list of ideas. At the end of a given time each person reads out his list thus generating stimuli for the rest of the group to produce some ideas.

Some practitioners prefer trigger sessions to the Osborn method and make them the central part of the brainstorming process, perhaps lasting up to an hour. The way in which the process may be integrated with other techniques will be examined in Section 5.9.

A strict time schedule should be set. For most people, ten ideas in five minutes is about right. The most fluent members of the group will produce anything up to thirty ideas but the atmosphere should still be relaxed rather than formal. If the trigger session is the first idea-generation procedure of the particular day's activities, a warm-up similar to that described in the previous section is desirable. If the format of Figure 5:5 is followed it should be modified to illustrate the principles of trigger sessions. The parallel between creativity tests and individual idea-generation can be pointed out; the importance of 'building' on the individual lists of ideas can also be emphasized. Short evaluating tests are suited and tests before and after introducing postponement of judgement can illustrate the two. This principle leads to increased numbers of ideas.

One advocate of trigger sessions uses a series of different coloured cards for the different stages of the meeting. Ideas produced by each member independently are written on cards of one colour; ideas developed subsequently by listening to the lists being read out are jotted down on cards of a different colour. This can be extended to other modifications of the technique (such as further stages under different conditions imposed by the leader). The cards can later help in evaluating the effectiveness of the modifications introduced.

Trigger sessions operate on the principle of introducing a certain amount of competitive pressure into the meeting. Some people perform better under some controlled level of stress, but others are uncomfortable and become resentful. When the stress is taken off, ideas sometimes flood into the mind as it relaxes. I have never deliberately tried this on a real problem, but in training sessions, the following device has also produced good results. A group of observers, watching a second group generate ideas, are asked to jot down their observations and any ideas that occur. The second group sees the problem in a fresh and detailed way, and produces a variety of ideas triggered by the working group. The second group may at the same time, however, have an inhibiting effect on the first one.

In general, there is less speculation in ideas coming out of a trigger session than is found in ideas from an Osborn-type brainstorming. Once again it seems expedient to work the group in short bursts – perhaps five minutes of individual thinking, followed by the period of building on the ideas being read out (which can take about two minutes and produces a dozen ideas for each member on average). Trigger sessions can operate for groups of as small as six because of the more individual nature of idea-generation but it can also operate for larger groups, up to about fifteen people. If Osborn and trigger-type brainstorming are to be run as part of the same exercise, the group can be split for the Osborn, and recombined for the trigger sessions.

5.6 RECORDED ROUND ROBIN ('6–3–5') (TECHNIQUE T.4.3)

A recent variation of the trigger session has developed in Europe. It is particularly suited for rather smaller groups, optimally six (for reasons explained below). It is another subroutine often following an Osborn-type warm-up, problem-redefinition and even idea-generation process.

Each member of the group receives a subproblem and three cards. He is asked to write the problem on each card, and then to think of one idea for each card. The cards are then passed to other members of the group according to some sort of system to ensure that one person is receiving different ideas, and as far as possible from different people. Each time the cards are exchanged, the last idea on each card is used as a stimulus to generate fresh or modified ideas. For six people it is possible to exchange the cards five times, according to the scheme outlined in Figure 5:7. In practice this does lead to some confusion if the organizer is not well-prepared, and even more complicated arrangements are necessary for groups other than of six people. Therefore the technique may be more conveniently operated in a truncated form with only two or three passes (as in Case Study 9). without a predetermined order of passing.

The method is now quite mechanical, and participants produce, in general, rather mundane and illogical ideas. For this reason, I prefer to introduce it as a means of control with a group that has become over-stimulated by an Osborn-type brainstorming into excessive fantasy and seems incapable of developing valuable and relevant ideas from the speculative concepts they have been generating.

Figure 5:7 *Recorded round robin: a scheme for passing on cards among a group of six people, for five rounds, so that no person passes an idea to the same person twice.*
Recorded round robin has been developed by practitioners in Germany and Holland. It is also known as 6:3:5, because in the full version the *six* people each convert *three* ideas and these are modified *five* times.

People	*Round 1*	*Round 2 1st pass to*	*Round 3 2nd pass to*	*Round 4 3rd pass to*	*Round 5 4th pass to*	*Round 6 5th pass to*
P1	P1	P6	P2	P5	P3	P4
P2	P2	P1	P3	P6	P4	P5
P3	P3	P2	P4	P1	P5	P6
P4	P4	P3	P5	P2	P6	P1
P5	P5	P4	P6	P3	P1	P2
P6	P6	P5	P1	P4	P2	P3

5.7 WILDEST IDEA (TECHNIQUE T.4.4)

The wildest idea subroutine is a systematic attempt by a brainstorming group to generate ideas from outrageous starting points that have already arisen in the course of the meeting. The rationale is exactly that of the wishful thinking subroutine of Chapter 4 – namely that an unusual starting point will help direct thoughts away from the conventional ideas that would in all likelihood have emerged in a more normal idea-generation session.

Although in a brainstorming group there is positive encouragement to develop wishful ideas ('hitchhiking'), the most speculative ideas often pass by unnoticed by everyone except the person who made the initial statement. If the leader recognizes that this is happening he can select a wild idea, or ask the group to do so, and request that the group continue brainstorming from that starting point. The customary result is for the group's ideas to become more practicable, but at the same time retaining an element of unexpectedness, by virtue of the unusual starting material.

The exact format of the wildest idea subroutine can be decided by the leader in the light of his understanding of the group (creative analysis). Among the options which he has at his disposal are group activities (Osborn-type brainstorming), trigger sessions, or recorded round robin. With an inexperienced group the last two options tend to direct the group too much into becoming more realistic in their thinking, and lead to evaluations during the brainstorming.

The following examples of wildest idea thinking were obtained recently:

> In a session on improving the works canteen, a brainstorming group became rather bogged down with thematic ideas relating to decor. When a wild idea was requested someone said 'have topless waitresses'. The hitchhiking was instantaneous, and produced an immediate joke – 'install a milk machine'. This proved more practicable than the idea which triggered it off, and also helped the group to get away from earlier lines of thought.
>
> In a different session, this time on utilizing waste material, the group had converged on a single line of attack, and had produced a large number of ideas on the principle of recycling the waste back into the system. The most promising idea, however, arose after a suggestion that the waste should be burned to heat the factory. One member of the group (the client) was able to recall that the company, an international one, had recently acquired a subsidiary with an interest in fire-lighters.

In the first example the wildest idea subroutine was introduced deliberately. In the second the use was spontaneous, clearly a more desirable state of affairs.

There is another situation in which a leader may decide to introduce wildest idea thinking. It is when the group has failed even to produce the starting stimuli of unusual ideas. In these circumstances he should first ask the group to try to imagine impossible but desirable starting concepts. Once a selection of these is obtained the procedure becomes similar to the ones described above. The two different approaches are illustrated in Figure 5:8.

Figure 5:8 When to use the wildest idea technique

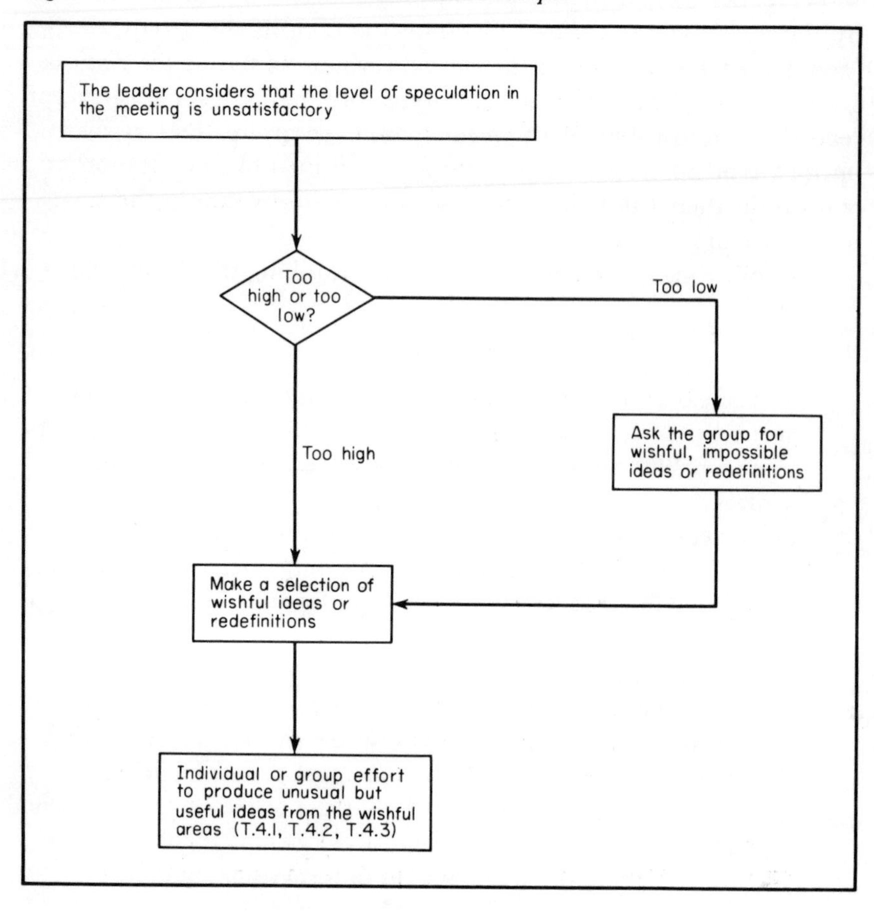

5.8 REVERSE BRAINSTORMING (TECHNIQUE T.4.5)

A second type of freewheeling may be needed after brainstorming activities, or in its own right. The situation sometimes arises when an idea has passed a preliminary evaluation, and when actions are about to be taken. If these actions are important and costly, or there are potentially serious consequences if something goes wrong, it is vital to minimize the risk of the unexpected. In such cases, reverse brainstorming can be tried.

Taking the defined set of actions as a starting point, the brainstorming group examines 'what might go wrong with this?' The group should include as many key personnel likely to be involved as possible, but should also include some disinterested outsiders. Evaluation of the results is relatively easy as an unanticipated but potentially dangerous problem is likely to be recognized by 'universal acclaim' during the meeting. One example of this is quoted in Case Study 5.

5.9 COMBINING THE ELEMENTS FOR GROUP IDEA-GENERATION SESSIONS

The closely interacting nature of the different subroutines has been indicated in the earlier sections. It should be remembered at all times that the actual idea-generation procedures are of little value without careful preparation of the group both before the meeting, and during the warm-up. Only then can subroutines be introduced with optimum chance of success. Only experience will tell the leader the approximate length of time for which 'his' groups can work optimally. (My own estimate is no longer than half an hour on a single subroutine and no longer than an hour and a half for the total idea-generation procedures. This may well be influenced by the style of the leader, as well as by the type of problem and composition of the group.) Each group tends to reach a certain level of speculation which will differ according to the procedures and the personalities involved. This will be reflected in the types of idea and their rate of production. The leader can modify the level of speculation as shown in Figure 5:9. Further understanding of this principle can be obtained by examining Case Study 14.

5.10 EFFECTIVE EVALUATION OF IDEAS FROM A BRAINSTORMING

At the end of a brainstorming session a large quantity of new data has been accumulated and noted. Before attempting to evaluate the data it is necessary to come to terms with important considerations regarding what a brainstorming can and cannot do. The material produced during an idea-generation session represents starting points

Figure 5:9 Uses of various modifications of brainstorming to vary the level of speculation of the ideas produced

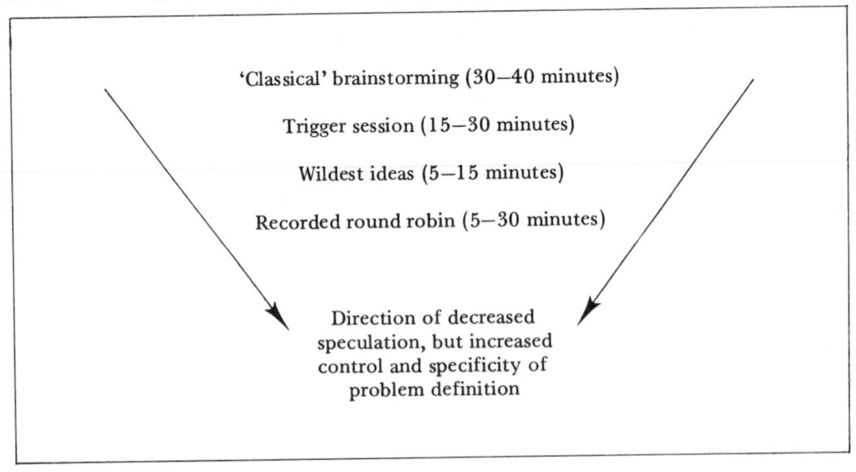

or opportunities which the agent can accept or reject. The attitude of the person intending to work on the problem will be a major factor in the subsequent utility of the brainstormed ideas. If he truly wants to solve a problem he will be receptive to some change in his perception of it, and the brainstorming exercise should provide that change. He will probably be most receptive to a stimulus the first time he receives it, and therefore is likely to recognize during the actual meeting the statements that he might ultimately develop and implement. Thus he should be asked to indicate his 'gut-feel' at the end of the meeting, and identify the ideas that seem the best starting points to complete solutions. (It may be objected that the agent's gut-feel could be misleading because of his overinvolvement; but this objection is based on a lack of appreciation of the elements that make an idea poor or good.)

If the agent does not think the idea is good, it immediately becomes somewhat inferior on these grounds. (Again in motivational terms, people motivate themselves, they work on what motivates them, not what others want to motivate them.)

Therefore it is preferable to leave the agent as much scope as possible to identify his solutions. If he is present in the meeting (a highly desirable state of affairs, although not advocated by all brainstorming practitioners) he is likely to start working on the idea he is most motivated to implement before receiving a formal report of the meeting. The report should then be a summary of the starting points identified by him. The new material can be circulated to the group so that they can clarify and expand any ideas they wish. The modified version should again go to the agent, but should not receive wider circulation until it has been reorganized, with the best ideas at the start of the document and the speculative ideas edited out but referred to for inspection if desired.

Reducing a list of several hundred items to a short-list is an example of a restructuring problem – morphological analysis can always be used (T.1.1) or a screening device as shown in Figure 3:5. It is often felt that such processes risk losing some good ideas. The consolation is that all that is being done is to make a rough separation of stimuli into a concentrated, potentially more valuable subset to be presented to the problem-solver, and the remainder.

5.11 SUMMARY

Although brainstorming is presented as a set of almost mechanical devices for groups involved in idea-generation activities the ideal situation for idea-generation would be one in which the principles of brainstorming are being obeyed, without the structure intruding. The different subroutines should be used flexibly, with such an understanding.

The actual idea-generation stage is in one sense less important than the preparation stages before it, and the evaluation stages afterwards. Given correct preparation, ideas will come without having to worry excessively about procedure.

Brainstorming can be complemented by an understanding and practice of restructuring, decision-aiding, and redefinitional techniques T.1, T.2 and T.3. When evaluating the ideas they should be regarded as stimuli to help an identified agent synthesize new possible solutions to his problem.

Chapter 6

Group Problem-solving: Synectics-type Subroutines

6.1 INTRODUCTION

Synectics is a term which has come to mean the practice of a set of procedures introduced and developed primarily by Synectics Inc., an American consultancy organization (see Appendix 2 for addresses of Synectics Inc. and Abraxas, the UK licensee). The name was coined by W. J. J. Gordon, a co-founder of the company, to describe a process leading to new insights through bringing together elements that are normally unrelated.

Synectics is a complex and rapidly changing body of knowledge and this account can in no way be considered a definitive one. The official sources mentioned above can be referred to for that. Rather I have concentrated on an approach which fits in with the principles of creative analysis based on personal experience and research over the period 1969–73. Much is owed to the writings of Gordon and Prince and my understanding of their philosophy and terminology, but the emphasis is my own, hence the chapter title.

6.2 ORIGINS

In 1961 W. J. J. Gordon summarized the results of over a decade of researches into creative individuals and the creative process. He suggested that individual creativity was associated with certain psychological states, which, if they could be induced, could increase the probability of creative breakthroughs. He transferred his attention from individuals to groups of people, because the communication process within a group could be recorded and studied for clues to the thinking which was going on. He also concentrated on technical problem-solving to provide more concrete criteria of success than might be obtained in artistic situations.

As the work progressed, Gordon became interested in attempting to reproduce the 'psychological states' systematically. In particular, he encouraged groups to attain a speculative mental state through the use of a variety of metaphoric and analogy procedures in a part of the meeting called the excursion.

In the next few years after publication of *Synectics* an important dimension was to be added to the technique by George Prince, working, initially, very closely with Gordon. Prince recognized that when people worked together in a group powerful forces operated which neutralized any creativity-spurring value which simple metaphoric procedures might have. Consequently, synectics began to develop ways in which groups of people would work together in a more efficient and productive way. The elements of synectics today can be traced back to the ideas of Gordon and Prince.

6.3 A FRAMEWORK FOR INTRODUCING SYNECTICS ELEMENTS INTO OPEN-ENDED PROBLEM SITUATIONS

There is an apparent complexity about synectics which can deter managers from studying it. The framework in Figure 6:1 presents the elements of synectics in stages requiring increasing levels of acceptance and application by the groups involved. The first stage consists of various simple procedures that can be introduced quite naturally during any discussion or meeting without prior approval by other members of the group.

If a practitioner is operating in a group which is prepared to adopt some synectics elements, he can later introduce important modifications to the structure of problem-solving meetings (stage 2), including role changes for the chairman and the person with the problem (the

Figure 6:1 *A framework for synectics experience.*
For an explanation of synectics terms see Section 6.4 and Appendix 1.

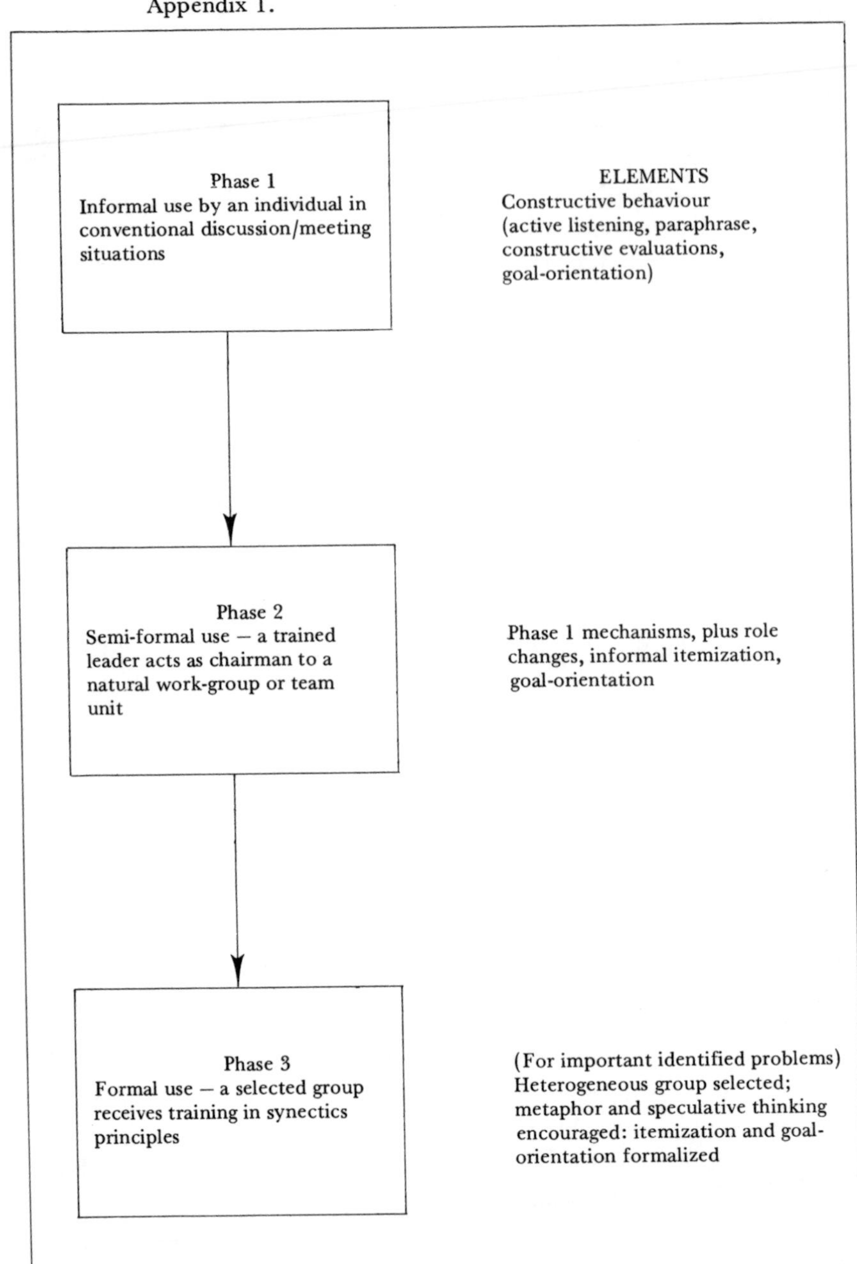

identified agent). The meetings can be seen as experimental situations, and synectics elements rejected or modified after they have been given a fair trial.

Given interest and acceptance of procedures tested in stages one and two, a group may elect to study synectics more thoroughly. 'Full-blooded' synectics has been described in books by Gordon (1961) and Prince (1970). Members of the group should read these books and gain experience as members of existing synectics teams and through attending training seminars.

The individual elements of synectics, in this framework, are shown in Figure 6:1.

6.4 ELEMENTS OF SYNECTICS

Broadly speaking the individual elements of synectics can be divided into

1 Techniques that foster constructive interpersonal relationships.
2 Processes that give the structure to a synectics meeting.
3 Roles that should be adopted by the participants.
4 Techniques designed to bring about an atmosphere conducive to creative thinking.

These elements are summarized in Figure 6:2 and considered, in turn, below.

Active listening

Active listening is a genuine attempt to increase the amount of information received during a discussion. It often happens that people do not take in all that is said to them. Typically, a group member listens most carefully at the start of a speaker's contribution and then with rapidly decreasing concentration as his own thoughts intrude. Unfortunately, the main information content may be presented during the period of inattentive listening. It is possible to make more effort to concentrate on the essence of a speech and this can be aided by showing that one has heard (feedback) and related it to one's own experience (paraphrase).

The effort is doubly productive, because one of the reasons why

Figure 6:2 Elements of synectics

Process	*Implications*
Constructive interpersonal behaviour	
Active listening	Increase your perception of other people's ideas and attitudes
Feedback	Show you have heard what has been said
Paraphrase	Show you have understood what has been said
Constructive structures within the meeting	
Itemization	Systematic treatment of each idea, statement or problem redefinition in a fair and constructive fashion. Careful records of all ideas and redefinitions must be kept during the meeting
Goal orientation	The attitude of mind which is constantly seeking new ways of looking at a problem (goal), and which accepts differences of opinion as expressions of different, but nonconflicting goals
Roles for a synectics meeting	
Leader	He is process not content oriented. He does not evaluate ideas nor does he spend time thinking up ideas of his own. His job is to enhance the effective operation of the group through his direction of the synectics process
Client (the person with the problem)	He is content not process oriented. He tries to be highly receptive to stimuli from the group as elements out of which he can develop new insights and solutions
Supportive group	Members try to provide evocative stimuli for the client. They are not concerned with learning concrete details from him, and therefore ask less questions but make more idea statements
Creativity-spurring processes	
Speculation, analogy/metaphor exercises	Both exercises encourage the creative rather than the analytic mode of thought. During an excursion the mind may be incubating the problem and on returning to the problem it is generally more relaxed and less constrained in producing original ideas

people talk in long monologues is fear that their main point is not being heard and understood. Justifications and repetitions are piled one on another in self-destructive profusion. Active listening enables group members to reassure the speaker that his point is taken and, more significantly, will allow them to develop his idea. It will also make them more effective presenters of ideas.

Feedback and paraphrase
As indicated above, a person in a group needs to know not only that he has been heard, but that he has been understood. Feedback reassures him on the former count, paraphrase on the latter.

To reinforce the point synectics practitioners sometimes preface their statements with 'So you are saying that . . .' or 'My understanding of your idea is . . .'

If the paraphrase is inadequate, at least the basis for a dialogue has been established. Although these devices seem 'obvious' they can have a profound effect on meetings. The person adopting them becomes recognized as being receptive and cooperative. His own ideas as a result receive more constructive attention. Just as negativity towards ideas breeds more negativity, active listening, feedback and paraphrase will lead to an overall improvement in attitudes and behaviour within a group.

*Goal orientation and the implications of asking questions**
Conventionally, when presented with a problem people try to learn as much as they can about it before attempting to suggest new ideas. Most educational and scientific training would support this method. It is basically the analytical and scientific approach. For close-ended problems it is not only correct but it is necessary, but there are other considerations in the open-ended group situation. Even when questions are asked with the legitimate intention of gathering information, they can accidentally put the expert or problem-solver on the spot.

'Have you tried reducing the speed of the motor?' is very easily interpreted as meaning 'Why haven't you tried reducing the speed?' It could also mean 'What do you think would happen if you reduced the speed of the motor?' but it is not easy to plan the precise impact of such a question.

---

*See also class T.3 (redefinitional aids) in Chapter 4.

Another reason why so many questions are asked in problem-solving sessions is excessive deference to the expert. He is expected to reject non-experts' suggestions quickly and so a non-expert has to build up his case gradually, in the hope of having a better chance of success that way. Thus, questions can lead to individuals working away on their own particular themes, instead of sharing them with the group. The group then inadvertently loses much of its potential ability to stimulate new ideas in the mind of the client. The questions evoke responses from the client which represent his view of the problem, and which thus include his prejudices and misconceptions. The group starts thinking like the client, along lines previously explored.

In group situations, the non-experts are advised to reduce the number of questions and substitute instead new ways of looking at the problem. In practice the client's response will be less constraining than his answer to a direct question, and more indicative of the novelty and potential value of the redefinition. A group moving towards more redefinitions and less questioning thus emphasizes the open-ended nature of the problem-solving situation (Figure 6:3).

As an example of the philosophy in practice, consider a dialogue between a sales manager, and a salesman with a poor performance record. The manager could start by asking: 'What are the latest sales returns for your region? Why are they always the lowest returns I get?'

He is unlikely to solve any problems, as he will have put the salesman on the defensive. Instead he might have said that the problem, as he saw it, was 'how to improve sales in a region that has a high percentage of corner-shop calls'. Further joint development of the problem might elicit more information about the unique nature of the salesman's problems, as the starting point is a neutral one, and does not put the junior man at a disadvantage.

With practice different types of goals will be recognized and freely produced during meetings. For example, there are goals which paraphrase someone's idea or need; goals which reflect individual experience or attitudes; goals which wish for utopian solutions, or develop through nonlogical stimuli; and goals which challenge boundary conditions. These can be compared with the redefinitional procedures (T.3) of Chapter 4. As a group develops its goal orientation it is increasing its ability to cope with open-ended problems.

Goal orientation as an attitude of mind can be practised quite

Figure 6:3 Questions and redefinitions

QUESTIONS

* may put the expert on the defensive

* may hide an idea which will not emerge, if the reply seems to reduce its value

* may direct the meeting towards previously explored areas

* may supply the rest of the group with the expert's view of the problem, reducing their capacity to suggest new approaches

* may indicate that the questioner wants information to work as an *individual*, building up a stronger case for a half-formed idea, instead of advancing it for *group* development.

REDEFINITIONS

* imply that the problem is an open-ended one

* that there are different ways of tackling it

* that the group can contribute useful ideas without having to think of the problem in the same way the expert does

* make it easier to establish novelty and potential value to the client.

IN A PROBLEM-SOLVING GROUP

QUESTIONS SEPARATE

REDEFINITIONS INTEGRATE

informally in any meeting. However, it is facilitated if a chairman encourages the reformulation of questions into new ways of looking at the problem. In so doing he has introduced an element of structure into the proceedings. If the chairman wishes to add more elements of synectics he can move towards phase 2 in the framework outlined in Figure 6:1.

Semi-formal use of synectics – itemization and role changes

In many problem-solving meetings the status of the chairman is high in organizational terms and this is reinforced by his role of imposing order or structure on the group. He can thus give excessive attention to his own ideas, and to those viewpoints coinciding with his own, while rejecting optional points of view. If this same person is one identified as the problem-solver, these personality factors become even more acute. The key change suggested and practised in synectics sessions is replacement of the chairman by a neutral-status *leader* who is concerned with the *process* of running the meeting, but does not contribute to the *content* by introducing ideas of his own. He is aware that the roles of the client and the supportive group are also rather different than those adopted in other meetings. The client is looking for new stimuli to help him see the problem in a new way, and as a result he must receive special attention; his reactions to redefinitions from the group must be noted. The supportive group (even if its members forget this) can best contribute by providing stimuli which they draw from their own experience. The leader should encourage them to present redefinitions and discourage them from asking excessive numbers of questions. Feedback, paraphrase, and goal orientation, in other words, should also be practised.

The leader can also introduce one of the elements of a more structured synectics to promote goal orientation and constructive evaluation of ideas. Typically an idea is considered as part of a close-ended system which is fixed and consequently satisfactory or unsatisfactory. Such an attitude is reflected in the response 'That won't work because . . .' A more constructive attitude would be to try to find out how the underlying concept might be modified to make it work. In recent synectics practice this philosophy has been incorporated into a procedure called *itemized response*. The person evaluating an idea (almost always the client) tries to list some of its good points before turning to its weaknesses (Figure 6:4). When this effort is genuine and incorporated into the evaluator's natural behaviour, he is moving towards becoming an intuitive practitioner of a very useful element of synectics.

The process can be illustrated by reference to Case Study 21. The problem was how to reduce fatal collisions between cars and lamp standards; the suggestion was to weaken the column so that it flew away on impact, and the immediate response was that the solution was a dangerous one to cars and pedestrians. If the problem had been examined using itemized response, the advantages of the method would have been clarified – namely that on theoretical grounds the

Figure 6:4 *Itemized response – evaluation of an idea as an open-ended concept.* Conventionally, an idea is evaluated in terms of why it will not work. Itemized response to an idea recognizes that it has valuable elements, and that those elements can be modified by the group, overcoming the weaknesses and thus modifying the idea (and the problem definition to which it is the solution). The negative elements can also be regarded as new subproblems for which fresh redefinitions can be formulated.

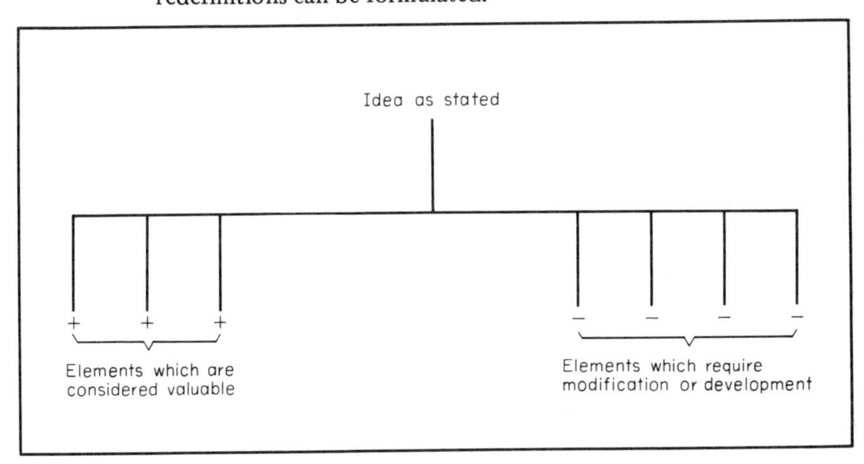

system would reduce deaths on impact. Then the objections could have been examined in terms of how to avoid the standard damaging other cars, and pedestrians. The modifications eventually adopted in the USA could then have been introduced into the argument (Figure 6:5).

Formal synectics meetings – speculative and metaphoric procedures
Within the framework described, most of the elements of synectics have been introduced in a relatively informal manner, which is as a result extremely flexible. However, most of the descriptions of the technique depict a group following a more formal procedure. One typical format is shown in Figure 6:6.

The group learns what type of solution is most likely to be accepted and is oriented towards the needs of the clients. The structure permits a thorough and systematic opening-up of the problem, and even rather reluctant clients will at least have every opportunity of seeing the problem in a new way. The imposition of such a structure inevitably reduces the level of speculation within the group, so that a procedure

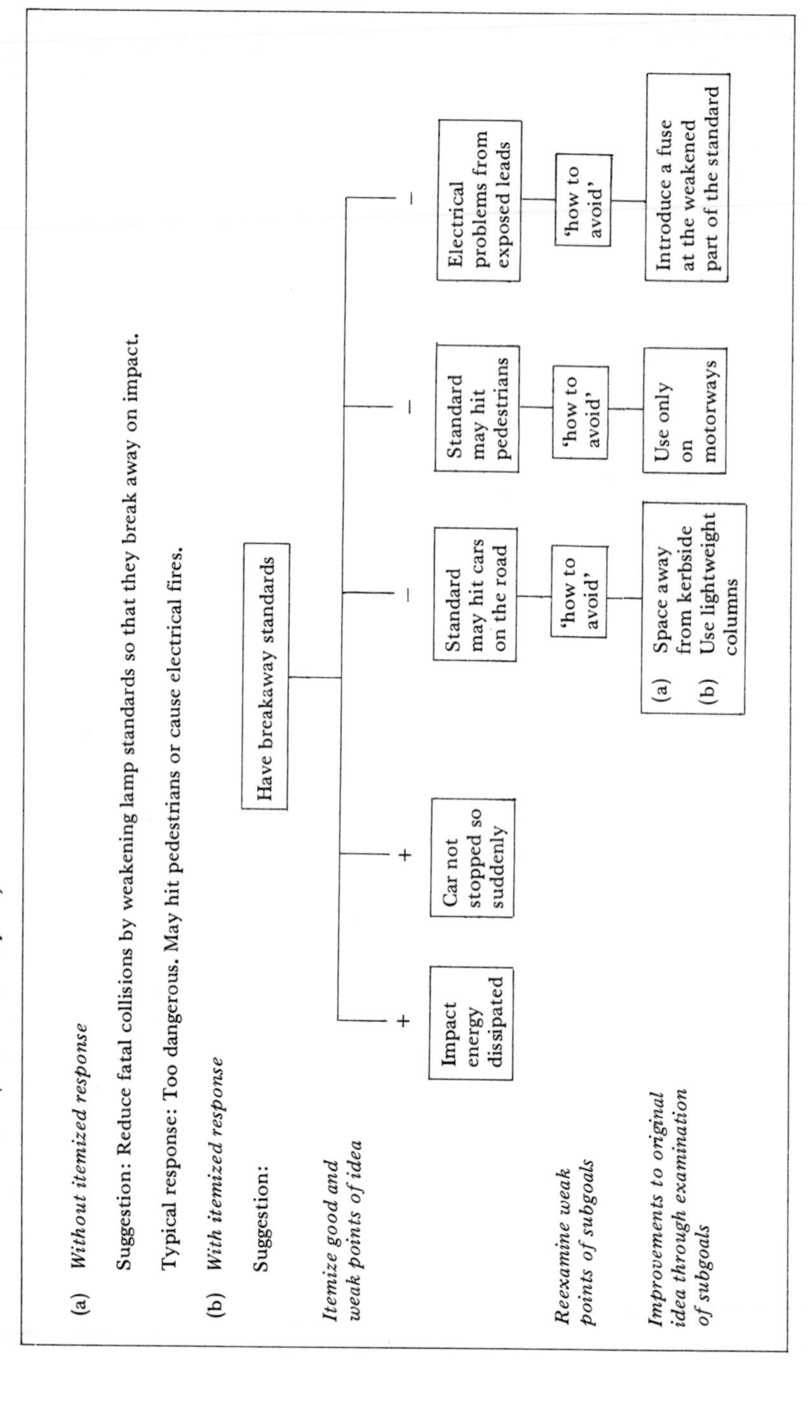

Figure 6:5 Examples of itemized response to a suggestion for reducing fatal collisions by the introduction of flyaway lamp standards (see Case Study 21)

Figure 6:6 *Format for a typical synectics session.*
The selection goals are examined sequentially. The procedure can be varied somewhat within each goal. In the illustration the second goal includes an excursion step. Five to fifteen minutes are spent on each goal, and the total meeting can take up to two hours. If the problem is important enough to need this complex structure, there is also often a need for several meetings.

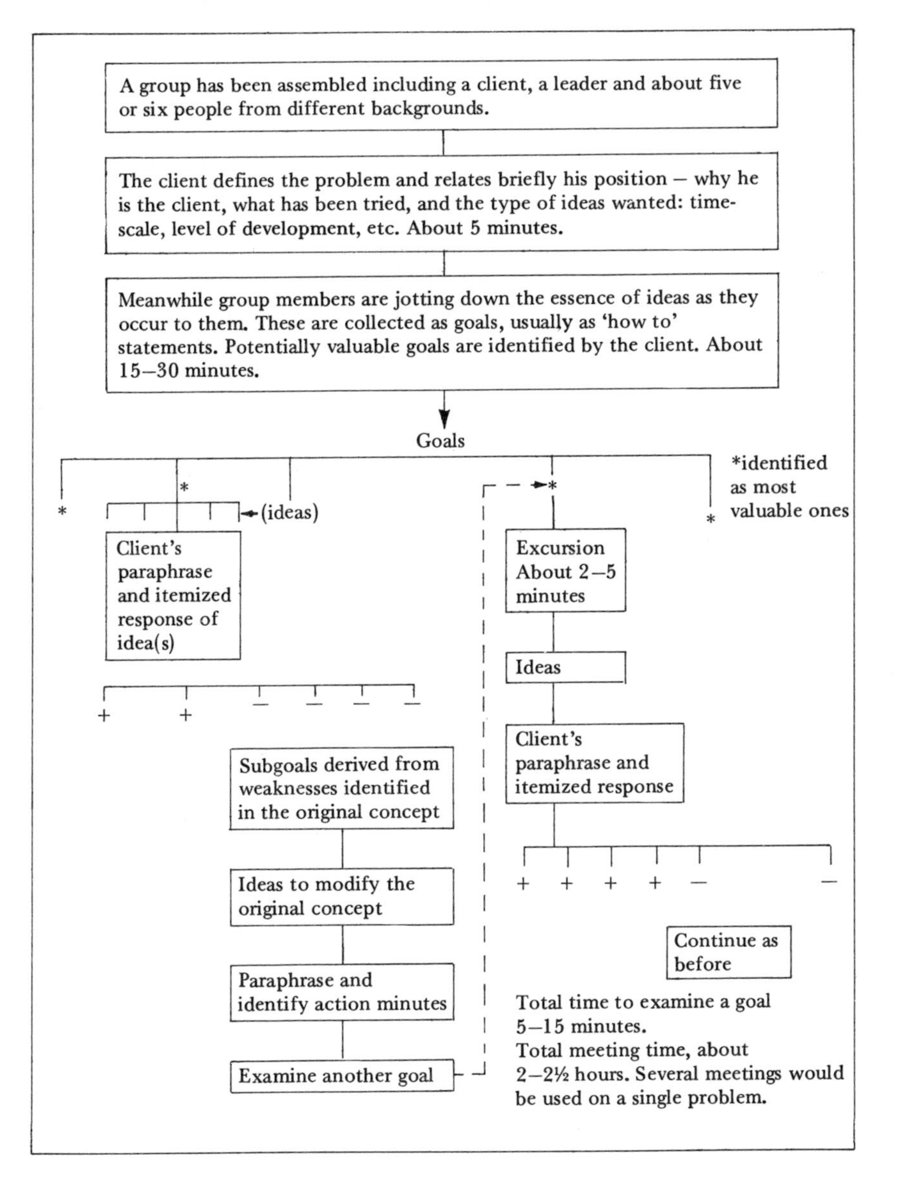

to increase speculation (the excursion) can be profitably introduced at some stage.

The excursion is a device for moving the group, at first, away from the problem into metaphoric speculations which directly stimulate new ideas (Figure 6:7). For groups with little experience of synectics, direct analogy is easiest to master, and the safest to introduce. As confidence grows, more demanding stages can be introduced. Although there is a recent trend against using excursions, experiments with groups in technical environments have regularly found value in the procedures, which should not be rejected out of hand for reasons of fashion. Examples of the individual elements of an excursion can be found in Case Study 1.

Creative people derive considerable pleasure from taking part in an excursion and this should not be allowed to overshadow the serious purpose behind it – to obtain new *but relevant* ideas. The leader should aim for the shortest excursion possible that seems to relax the group and take them away from the problem, and then concentrate on a gradual return to reality. The process is represented in Figure 6:8, and illustrated in Case Study 1.

6.5 IMPLEMENTATION OF IDEAS

As with brainstorming, synectics is criticized for the apparent difficulties encountered in progressing ideas. There is certainly no formula which makes the process easy, although progression can be made a little less difficult by attention to correct problem selection and client identification at the outset of the exercise. ('Volunteered' clients, for example, may have hidden reasons for rejecting any ideas produced in a session.)

During the actual session, wherever possible, the final stage in evaluating a possible solution should include identifying actions which the client has to take to validate the possible solution. If the client has to report back to the group he will have an additional motivation to complete the validation steps.

In establishing possible solutions during the meeting, every concept can usefully be tested against three criteria:

1 Is it novel (to the client)?

Figure 6:7 The principal factors influencing the leader's decisions during an excursion

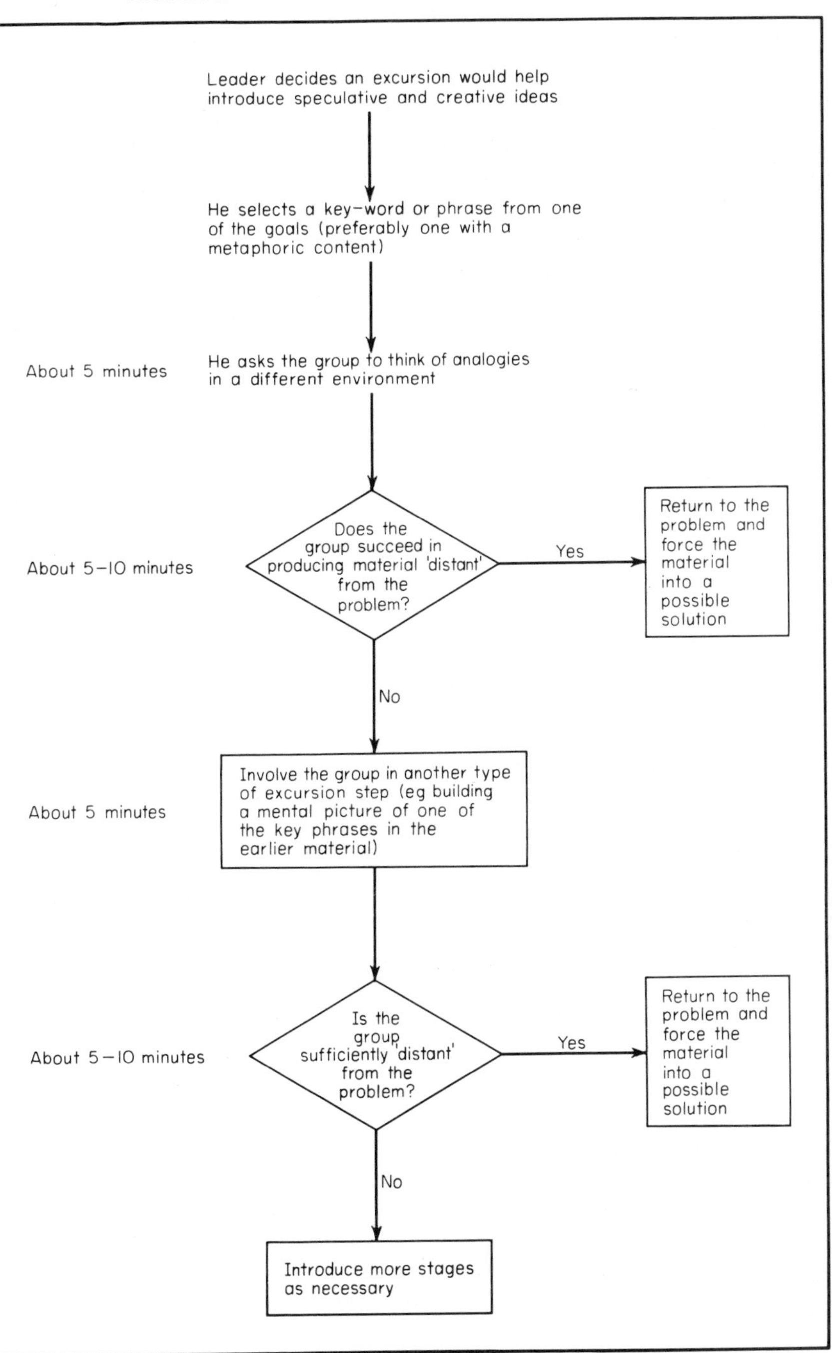

Figure 6:8 *An excursion seen as a device for changing the level of speculation during a synectics meeting.*

A Rapid return to reality – poor use of speculative level attained in the excursion. The concept is likely to be similar to those obtained before the excursion.

B More gradual return to reality – better use of the speculative level attained during the excursion. The concept is more likely to be distant from those obtained before the excursion.

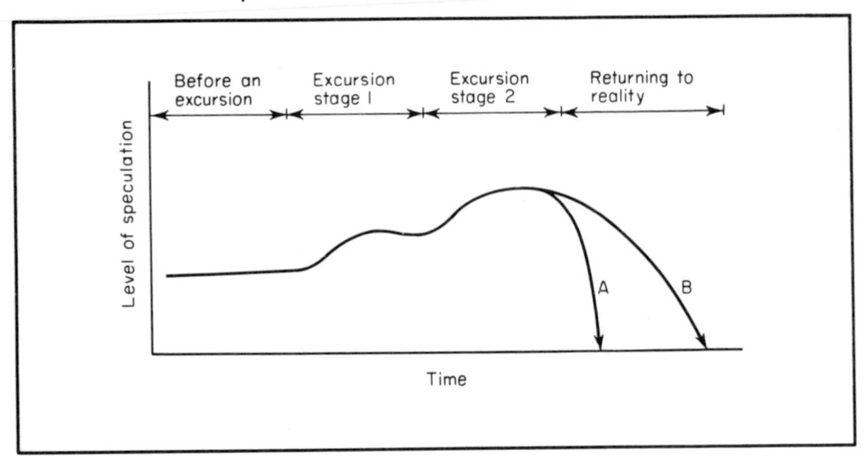

2 If it works, will it solve some relevant problem definition?
3 Can the client validate it within his perceived time constraints?

Unless a concept satisfies these criteria, it is likely to be yet another redefinition in disguise, and should be recorded as such.

Rapid reporting of the meeting helps progress the ideas, especially if the client is prepared to cooperate in the activity. (Lack of interest on his part is a sign of poor motivation.) The key points of the report should be the possible solutions as paraphrased by the client. A complete list of redefinitions and information about excursion procedures are probably best relegated to an appendix.

6.6 SCOPE OF SYNECTICS

To most people who have read of the technique, synectics is synonymous with technical innovation. However, in America the technique has been applied successfully in administration, marketing, personnel management, production, research, cost-reduction, process improvement, and most frequently in the area of new product development. Groups in Europe have involved housewives, children and various other untrained participants. In the UK one specific operating group studied over twenty technology-oriented problems; nearly thirty problems related to new-product development, and about a dozen miscellaneous business advertising and market-research-type problems during the period 1969 to 1971. A majority of these clients considered that the technique had been of some value, and felt that the changes in the leader role and the importance of behavioural aspects (such as feedback and spectrum — see Appendix 1) were the most valuable elements. About half the sample also considered that excursions had been useful in the meetings.

Almost all the reported exercises involved full-blown meetings incorporating most of the elements described in Section 6.4. No doubt further work will identify more clearly which situations are best suited for such a formal application of the technique, but in comparison there are far more opportunities for the introduction of synectics rather informally into managerial practice. For example, in setting up management by objectives or job enrichment exercises improved exchanges of views might occur if more attention is paid to goal orientation by each party involved. In general, whenever one is asked to make an evaluation of an idea or course of action, a brief itemization can be of value; in attempting to communicate, active listening, feedback and paraphrase will establish confidence.

As a manager increases his informal synectics skills he will become aware of more and more work areas where he can use them to advantage.

6.7 SELECTION AND TRAINING FOR SYNECTICS

What level of preliminary training is necessary for a manager to acquire informal synectics skills for himself and subsequently introduce them to other members of his organization? My personal experience suggests that managers have been able to understand the underlying principles through private study and experiment with a minimum of instruction. Such self-taught practitioners will be best placed for subsequent professional instruction. These managers will benefit from regular contact with other synectics practitioners and also with groups covering peripheral skills of a behavioural nature, such as local encounter groups, the Association of Humanistic Psychology, etc.

The training department of a firm is in a rather different position. Here, certainly, professional advice before starting and as a monitoring function will accelerate the process of developing a package suited to an organization's specific needs. Nevertheless, training officers are accustomed to studying and introducing new materials, and creative problem-solving, with its emphasis on synectics-type procedures, should prove feasible and valuable in many training situations.

Gordon originally suggested that a full-time synectics group should be selected after a long interview with each member lasting several days, to attempt to build up a list of people with complementary skills.

This method does not seem to have been adopted in practice, often because a manager may wish to introduce synectics methods into an on-going team. Provided this team is sympathetic to the technique an on-going problem-solving group can be maintained by building up a panel of additional participants. These should be cultivated by inviting people who show interest in the technique to take part in meetings, and by maintaining contact with those who have a constructive effect, even in their first meetings.

On occasions there will be a need for groups with specified backgrounds (see Case Studies 11, 12 and 13) but for problem-solving groups in general the backgrounds should be as diverse as possible, consistent with an understanding of the broad implications of the problem. For technical problems an engineer, a physical chemist, a technical manager, and technical sales executives would be a diverse and suitable mixture of specialities.

As might be expected, performance on creativity tests does not give sufficient information to select or reject someone for a synectics group. Creativity tests can take various forms. They are intended as research tools to help uncover various thinking processes, especially original thinking. The tests mentioned in Figure 5:5 and Case Study 12 are modified versions of the Torrence tests. These measure the capacity of subjects to produce large numbers of ideas (fluency), to produce different types of ideas (flexibility), and to produce rare and unusual responses when compared with ideas of other people (originality).

Because many extraneous factors influence creativity the tests must be administered in conjunction with other research measures and even then the results may not accurately predict creative potential of the subject.

There is increasing evidence that a group working well and creatively does not have to contain a large number of highly creative individuals. In fact, an excess of these might inhibit each other, so if one is available, the group might benefit from additional members who are providers rather than creators – in other words people with good listening skills and interpersonal behaviour traits.

The most frightening role, to the manager learning synectics, is that of leader. It is difficult only in the sense that the more sessions one conducts, the better one becomes. As consolation, however, the trainee should accept that there is a robustness about group meetings, and that honest attempts to improve their operation will have a positive effect on, and often a high level of sympathetic cooperation from, the other group members.

6.8 RELATIONSHIPS BETWEEN A GROUP PRACTISING SYNECTICS AND THE REST OF THE ORGANIZATION

Because synectics makes sense, there is a natural tendency for regular practitioners to want to spread the gospel. However, it is not easy to demonstrate that the application of a technique has had a direct impact on an organization's operations (not to mention its profits) and therefore it is prudent to view synectics as a means to the longer-term goals of improving the functioning of managers in formal and informal meetings, thus indirectly contributing to the company's innovative output. A low-profile approach will reduce suspicion towards an apparently gimmicky device for problem-solving.

Internal training courses, with as much support as possible from senior managers, can help win acceptance far better than memoranda or reports. The technique has to be experienced before it can be fairly evaluated. These educational ploys will also provide the synectics group with clients who can then recognize a real opportunity for successful problem-solving applications in their work situations. Before accepting such proposals, the contact man in the synectics group will have to decide if the problem is suited for group problem-solving techniques (see Figure 1:11) and more likely to benefit from synectics than brainstorming (see Figure 5:1). He should also determine the chances of success and successful implementation of ideas, and try to identify key personnel who will have an influence on the problem-solving situation. In keeping with the low-profile attitude recommended, it should be emphasized that a synectics group is not in the business of solving other people's problems – rather it exists to help people solve their own problems more creatively and efficiently.

This is the foundation for a good and symbiotic relationship with the host organization. The rewards of the group must be sought outside those of the conventional problem-solver to reduce suspicion of parasitic tendencies. If patents result from a meeting, the logic of the situation demands that the expert be recognized as sole inventor because in a correctly assembled group there will be no one else likely to distinguish a true innovative concept from a flight of fancy.

In these ways a synectics group will avoid some of the dangers of alienating themselves from the rest of the organization and pave the way for wider acceptance of the procedures.

6.9 SUMMARY

Synectics is a body of experience which can be introduced by individuals or groups in formal or informal problem-solving meetings and discussions. It includes procedures for improving interpersonal behaviour in groups, and procedures for increasing the creative potential of individuals and groups.

The exact way in which these elements are used must be determined by the individual practitioner through a consideration of his specific environment and problem-solving needs.

Chapter 7

Creative Analysis of Some Real Problems

Over the period April 1972 to May 1973 managers attending seminars on creative analysis at Manchester Business School were invited to bring along problems from their own work situations which they had identified as open-ended as defined in Chapter 1. A significant proportion of managers brought problems that seemed completely close-ended. In each of these cases, which were studied during the seminars, redefinition techniques transformed the close-ended problem into an open-ended one. A typical problem was 'Should I be doing X or Y'. After redefinition, other possibilities emerged such as a new option Z, modified X or Y, or combinations of X and Y.

In an even greater proportion of cases the problem was instantly or rapidly established as being outside the sphere of influence of the alleged agent. Thus there may be a strong tendency for managers to believe that it is their responsibility to solve problems which either more correctly 'belong' to someone else, or, at best, are situations which call for problem-solving groups and specialist techniques.

The problems shown in Figure 7:1 are typical (except for the absence of close-ended problems) and are the first five that were submitted on a recent course. The managers were in the middle layers of their organizations. One can follow the decision-making process shown in Figure 1:4 to establish a line of attack. The analyst considers the main aspects outlined in Section 1.4 – the agent and

Figure 7:1 A selection of open-ended problems submitted during a problem-solving seminar

Problem 1	How can I motivate a group of older employees who see no advancement and are working out time before retiring?
Problem 2	How should we treat a brilliant scientist who does not believe anyone else can get good ideas? He is a senior manager and, because of the commercial success of one of his ideas, has power beyond his status in planning meetings.
Problem 3	How can I improve the effectiveness of this production line?
Problem 4	How can consumers be persuaded that our product is as good functionally as the opposition, which just has a better image, but is the dominating market leader?
Problem 5	How can I persuade our directors to accept the recommendations we have drawn up for them?

his sphere of influence; selection of creative and analytical procedures; and relative merits of individual and group techniques.

7.1 PROBLEM 1: MOTIVATING OLDER PERSONNEL

A good example of a problem which is outside the control of the person who brought it. Just as proponents of creative analysis argue that people work best on ideas they have helped develop, so motivational theorists believe that people motivate themselves. In the absence of the people themselves, their managers can only think of the opportunities and hope for the best results when the actual people are introduced to the ideas.

The problem might be redefined in terms of 'How can I compel . . .', when it becomes meaningful (if not necessarily desirable!), but for acceptance and implementation the key personnel themselves should be involved in the idea-generation stages.

This analysis suggests that a group technique which encourages the production of ideas might be used. Synectics and brainstorming have been successfully utilized on similar problems.

In one instance, blue-collar workers within a large American retail store were trained in synectics and demonstrably improved their understanding of their own and their colleagues' problems and relationships. A subproblem – how to motivate Jack to get to work on time – became redefined as how to enable Jack to work more flexible hours (because of his family commitments, Jack could not start work until his children had been delivered to their schools).

In a different (UK) exercise a service section within an industrial organization again seemed demotivated. A series of synectics sessions indicated that there were several possible ways of 'enriching' their jobs, but in each case the change threatened their long-term security of employment. Here the synectics sessions did not solve the problem but indicated that wider organizational implications had to be taken into consideration. More success could be gained by involving the group with the decision-making echelons of higher management – the more appropriate agents. This would in all probability have been overlooked without involving the people.

Professor Herzberg, a leading exponent of motivational theory, has also resorted to group idea-generation in such situations. He favours brainstorming, and then separates out the ideas which are potentially motivating from those which are merely removers of dissatisfaction ('hygiene factors').

7.2 PROBLEM 2: COPING WITH THE BRILLIANT SCIENTIST

This problem was posed by a line manager concerned with personnel development, who believed he was relating a problem common to himself and his senior colleagues. This problem is even more beyond the sphere of influence of the person stating it. The scientist himself probably would not accept that there is any problem at all.

In the absence of the scientist any problem-solving activity is likely to be barren, or at best short term. The results of such activities will rely on his acceptance of any suggested course of action (as will, by a similar argument, the results of this analysis).

Once again the man has to be helped to help himself. Creative group techniques are suggested. One company ran a course on the communication aspects of synectics in a disguised effort to change the behaviour of one of its senior people. This experiment is still in progress, although this sort of action seems most in keeping with the principles laid down in this book.

Using another of the techniques (reversals), the problem falls within the sphere of influence of the group of people concerned if it is redefined as 'How do we organize ourselves to improve our relationships with the scientist'.

7.3 PROBLEM 3: IMPROVING THE EFFECTIVENESS OF A PRODUCTION LINE

The person who brought the problem was able to implement changes to the production line. He therefore could be said to have adequate control over the problem so that an individual problem-solving process can be attempted in the first instance.

A production line is a good example of a complex and dynamic situation which could be split into smaller units for initial restructuring of the problem. Attribute listing or morphological analysis might be a suitable starting point.

Specific areas could then be isolated for attention. The problem is open-ended, and in practice this is one of the few types of problems which are regularly tackled by groups using creativity-spurring techniques and in particular brainstorming. There is no contradiction with the statement in the first paragraph – the agent can make a reasonable attempt to tackle the problem, and having increased the efficiency to the best of his ability he can call in a multi-discipline group.

Such groups, generally called value analysis or value engineering, often make spectacular alleged savings. In two recent exercises one firm saved £200 000 and £500 000 respectively, from groups meeting approximately twice a month over an eight-month period. Such exercises run all the smoother if there has been a creative analysis which identifies key personnel able to contribute. Too often the group, although more productive than any individual, does not include a sufficiently wide cross-section of people. Two examples will illustrate this point.

The first involved a firm of solvent manufacturers which began a project to improve safety conditions. A working party of technical managers met regularly, but at the end of the project the ideas were screened by members of their own fire-fighting security group, who should have been invited to join the group in the first instance.

The second example, from a different company, is concerned with a conventional value analysis exercise on a production line. After nearly a year, two basic strategies had been identified, representing potential savings of a quarter and a half-million pounds respectively. The higher-figure strategy was rejected by the board, on the grounds that it 'might cause industrial action that would result in losses in excess of the savings envisaged'. A decision based on more concrete evidence could have been made, if the ideas team had included representatives from different levels in the organization so that potential objections could have been anticipated earlier.

7.4 PROBLEM 4: PERSUADING CONSUMERS

As with motivating, so with persuading. In the absence of the consumers no real situation can be implemented, so the problem is outside the sphere of influence of the person who brought it along to the seminar. This is a close-ended attitude frequently found in technical departments, which operate on the principle that anything which can improve a product will inexorably help sell it.

Application of creative analysis suggests that consumers should be involved as illustrated in the case studies of Chapter 10. The problem is open-ended and involves groups. I would favour synectics here. The result will probably lead to an appreciation of other definitions such as 'How can we build into our product what consumers like in the opposition's product'.

7.5 PROBLEM 5: PERSUADING SENIOR MANAGERS

Again there seems to be a close-ended view of an essentially open-ended group situation. Creative analysis suggests that the manager or team making recommendations should attempt to involve the senior managers more completely at an earlier stage. As with the consumers, synectics might be one way to facilitate such a dialogue – particularly involving itemized response towards ideas, thus modifying the idea in a way which makes it more acceptable to the decision-making echelons of the company.

7.6 SUMMARY

In the above problems I have tried to show how the principles of creative analysis and specific aids to problem-solving can be applied to real-life management situations.

A brief analysis in terms of key agents, sphere of influence, need for creative and analytical solving inputs, and individual or group activity will help direct the entire course of the problem-solving process.

The manager who wishes to take his problem-solving seriously could add to this a retrospective analysis of the impact of the problem-solving process by keeping records as indicated in Chapter 1. He can further monitor his efforts by comparing them against the case studies in the subsequent chapters.

PART TWO

CREATIVE ANALYSIS IN PRACTICE

Introduction to Part Two

A case study is a report of a specific set of events, presented to the reader in as unbiased a way as possible so that he can draw his own conclusions about how the situation arose, and the merit of the procedures adopted by the people described in the study.

It is inevitable that case examples are to some degree biased as they have been selected to illustrate particular points. In these cases the criteria for selection have been:

1 That the situation is likely to have general interest.
2 That each case illustrates a manager or group tackling an open-ended problem situation with procedures described in Part One.
3 That the description can illustrate the problem-solving principles without divulging information which the people concerned might prefer to remain confidential.

In a few instances background information has been slightly modified to disguise situations which might otherwise embarrass the principals involved.

The recommended use of case study material is for discussion. A few notes have been added to the more complex cases to relate them to the procedures introduced in Part One. However, there is no one correct interpretation of any historical document, and the reader should make his own analysis of each study before going on to read the notes.

Chapter 8

Case Studies from a Technically-based Group using Structured Techniques for Open-ended Problem-solving

8.1 BACKGROUND INFORMATION

The central R and D laboratory of a major UK company contains a specialist group with a general 'opportunity-seeking' brief. To this end, experience in general principles of creativity has been built up since about 1967. There is a commitment to maintain an expertise in organizing problem-solving activities and regular brainstorming and synectics sessions are held at which the responsibility for organizing, and the actual leadership, rotate through the entire group. At any time at least one member has received additional training by attending courses held outside the company.

For some years the group has offered problem-solving facilities to the various divisions of the company. A small number of tangible results have emerged (for example, a new product idea test-marketed in 1971) but by 1973 the members of the group had concluded that the true value of their expertise was less tangible. They felt that they were acting as catalysts within the research and development division, helping technical personnel to become more company-oriented.

The group leader was directly responsible to the technical director, and informal access to other divisions was encouraged. The group had considerable licence from the technical director in their choice of projects. Compared to other technical managers, members of the group had good prospects for promotion or transfer to other parts of the business. Elsewhere in the laboratory, colleagues tended to view the group with some suspicion, possibly because of its informal position and lack of evidence of success. However, serious public-relations exercises in all major divisions had exposed a good cross-section of middle managers to techniques such as synectics. Managers who had actually worked with the group tended to be more favourably disposed, and often maintained regular contacts.

In 1971 the attitudes of clients who had worked with the group were assessed by a small survey. The members of the sample had all commissioned a synectics or a brainstorming session within a year of the survey. The survey form for synectics is shown in Figure 8:1; the form for brainstorming was similar. Most clients considered that the techniques had helped them (Figure 8:2) and had some impact on their subsequent treatment of the problem and that the synectics procedures all had some value (Figure 8:3).

The following case studies illustrate the working procedures of the group.

8.2 CASE STUDY 1: INVENTING A PROCESS FOR MONITORING EFFLUENT

In 1970 a company within the parent organization commissioned the R and D laboratory to help them achieve a more precise monitoring of grease levels at a checkpoint in an effluent flow within the manufacturing process. The existing method employed a simple dip-can; samples were removed from the stream at regular intervals. The grease particles varied considerably in composition and size with time, and the analysis figures were suspect. An engineer (the client) within the R and D department examined the problem in consultation with the ideas group. None of the methods to hand seemed adequate, and the team accepted that they would have to design a novel system for monitoring the grease. The best solution came out of a synectics session, organized and conducted as follows.

Figure 8:1 Survey form on the value of synectics

In . . . . you took part in a synectics session on . . . .

. . . .

Remembering as best you can what took place in that meeting, please answer the following questions by indicating in the appropriate box which of the possibilities most closely corresponds to your opinion.

Question 1

To what extent do you think the ideas contributed to your insight into the problem?

not at all ☐ a little ☐ some ☐ a great deal ☐

Question 2

To what extent did the session influence your subsequent treatment of the problem?

not at all ☐ a little ☐ some ☐ a great deal ☐

Question 3

Some aspects of the technique can be used in other group activities. In your opinion, how would the introduction of the following changes influence the efficiency of meetings you attend?

Figure 8:1 – continued

Change	*Effect on Efficiency*						
	a great decrease	some decrease	a small decrease	no change	a small increase	some increase	a great increase
A synectics-type leader writing up all ideas in front of the group.	☐	☐	☐	☐	☐	☐	☐
The group following the synectics principles of good listening, positive reaction to ideas and noncompetitive behaviour.	☐	☐	☐	☐	☐	☐	☐
The group thinking of the problem in terms of metaphors and analogies at some stage during the meeting.	☐	☐	☐	☐	☐	☐	☐
Postponing judgement of fanciful and speculative ideas in order to increase chances of creative ideas being produced.	☐	☐	☐	☐	☐	☐	☐

Question 4

Do you have any other observations about synectics, or qualifications to any of your answers above?

Figure 8:2 *Response to questions 1 and 2 of the survey.*
16 brainstorming clients were polled, and 20 synectics clients.

	Brainstorming		*Synectics*	
	Insight	*Impact*	*Insight*	*Impact*
Number of respondents classifying the technique:				
Of no value	0	1	0	1
Of little value	3	3	8	5
Of some value	10	8	11	12
Of high value	3	4	0	2

Figure 8:3 *Response to question 3 of the survey*

	Process-oriented leader	*Structure to improve group behaviour*	*Use of metaphor*	*Encouragement of speculation and fantasy*
Number of respondents classifying the element as having:				
A high negative effect	0	0	0	0
A medium negative effect	1	0	1	1
A low negative effect	0	1	2	1
No effect	2	1	4	2
A low positive effect	6	1	5	5
A medium positive effect	4	7	8	7
A high positive effect	6	9	0	4

Problem-solving team

The team was made up of six people: three members of the ideas group, the engineer and a colleague, plus one outsider from a different division. The members had different background training and job responsibilities.

The three members who were inexperienced in synectics received, before the meeting, a descriptive handout which was about two pages long and gave a general introduction to the principles and procedures of the technique.

The synectics meeting

The engineer began by outlining the problem for about five to ten minutes. The rest of the group tried to understand it and redefine it in their own words. All redefinitions and possible solutions were recorded on flipcharts.

At the start of the analysis, the problem was defined as 'How to take a representative sample from a large mass of fluid for grease analysis'.

Typical redefinitions by the synectics team were:

1 How to meter the effluent without taking a sample.
2 How to measure the density of the effluent.
3 How to obtain a continuous representative sample and metering proportional to the flow rate.

In addition, within ten minutes from the start of the session a possible solution had been suggested based on emulsifying the effluent and measuring turbidity. The client was asked to evaluate the idea. He said that it was a new approach as far as he was concerned, but that it could not be validated easily within the time at his disposal.

At this stage the leader decided that fresh ideas would be obtained more easily after a metaphoric examination (excursion) rather than through pursuing the turbidity idea any further. The group leader was questioned about procedure after the meeting. He felt that it was almost obligatory to 'go into an excursion' during a synectics session, and the ideas group had always operated that way. Later (about 1972) they began experimenting with modified versions of the technique which did not include these metaphoric steps.

However, the consensus of opinion remained that an excursion would still be of value for technical problems, where new insights are required, and for groups who have worked together for a long period.

Excursion

The material generated to that point (which had been written up on flipcharts) was removed from the view of the group. The leader took as his starting-point one of the key words from the original definition – *sample*. He asked the members of the group to call out anything they could think of which might be considered samples from the world of astrophysics. Among the five or six ideas generated were:

1 Moon-rock
2 Urine
3 Bacterial counts on astronauts

Then the group went into a second stage of the excursion, attempting to identify with part of the problem. The leader asked what it felt like to be a bacterium on an astronaut. The responses noted on the flipchart included the following:

1 I've stopped multiplying.
2 I am aware for the first time that I am being observed.
3 I'm still multiplying fast – I like the oxygen.
4 I didn't ask to come, but now I've acquired an appetite for speed. I like the view.

After about five minutes, the group examined the material and tried at the request of the leader to summarize the material in an evocative and concise form. The following five statements were obtained:

1 Flight of fancy
2 Latent hunger
3 Repulsive hero
4 Passive pioneer
5 Pioneering stowaway

'Passive pioneer' was then taken as a starting point for a further stage in the excursion. This time the leader requested examples of passive pioneers from the world of the Arctic. Examples produced were:

1 Husky dogs
2 Penguins
3 Spiders
4 Rats
5 Nuclear submarines
6 Icebergs

The group was now nearing the end of the excursion, and as a last stage the members developed information about one of these examples – spiders. The following collection of both mundane and evocative facts was obtained:

> They have eight legs, eat smaller insects, spin webs which are sticky to trap prey. Small harmless specimens generate fear. Ubiquitous symbols of perseverance, neglect and decay. They move in as soon as people leave. Their webs are horrible when dry, but beautiful when wet. In folklore they have power to arrest bleeding. A spider can spin a silky life line to escape, when you are cutting it with scissors.

Development of ideas from the metaphoric material of the excursion
At this stage the group referred back to the original problem and simultaneously examined the information about spiders. The concept of a spider's web seemed immediately relevant and the group descended to reality via an initially speculative statement. The steps in this process were as follows:

> Step 1. Trap grease on a spider's web.
> Step 2. Use a web or mesh of material that attracts grease.
> Step 3. Use a strip of polyester fabric as the mesh to trap all the grease.

The client confirmed that this was a starting point for a possible solution in that it satisfied criteria of novelty, feasibility and testability. The group was to return to the concept later in the meeting and develop it still further. In its final form, the idea submitted to the engineer became:

> Remove all oil from a continuous sample by deposition on to a large lipophilic surface such as polythene, polyester or treated glass fibre. This could either collect all grease in the sample to give an integrated total over a given time-period, or the lipophilic surface could be in the form of a strip moving through the effluent sample to give a continuous record of the grease concentration.

Before developing this idea (which proved to be the one eventually used by the client) other possibilities were also derived from the material of the excursion. The final list of optional approaches provided by the group to the client included a continuous centrifugation of the sample stream; colorimetric or radiometric monitoring of a tracer material which reacted with grease; and turbidity measurements after emulsifying the sample stream by mechanical, chemical or ultrasonic techniques.

The client accepted the 'spider's web' option as the most promising line of attack. Later, while examining the patent literature he found a process from another country which was similar to the design he intended to assemble, and which he was able to submit to the management of the factory.

8.3 CASE STUDY 2: GENERATION OF CONCEPTS FOR CONSUMER PRODUCTS

In 1970 members of the ideas group worked on a joint project with a research team which wanted to develop a list of concepts for new consumer products within a defined area of search. The market researchers were concerned with developing the products further for their clients; the ideas group were additionally interested in developing their methods for generating new product concepts.

At the outset it was agreed to test several techniques for generating ideas, and to examine means of reducing the numbers to manageable proportions through subsequent consumer testing.

A panel fo 12 people agreed to take part in the exercise: four members of the ideas group, three members of the client group (the market researchers), and five additional participants from other parts of the company. The panel included a scientist, technologists, development managers, market researchers and housewives. Except for one or two absences for unavoidable reasons, all participants took part in a normal type meeting, at least one synectics session and a brainstorming session. In addition, a morphological analysis had been made, and the problem represented on a matrix. Each participant was given a portion of the matrix and asked to generate ideas with the cells of the matrix. The synectics activities were separated into two sessions. Each of the sessions had a different leader from the ideas group who attended as a participant at the second session. The compositions of the different meetings are shown in Figure 8:4.

Figure 8:4 Composition of the idea-generating meetings

Meeting	*Total number of participants*	*Number of participants from the market research group (client)*	*Number of participants from the ideas group*	*Number of other participants*
Formal meeting	11	2	4	5
Synectics 1	6	1	3	2
Synectics 2	7	1	3	3
Brainstorming	10	1	4	5
Morphological analysis	9	2	3	4
Number of different participants taking part in exercise	12	3	4	5

Formal meeting

The first session was similar to the sort of meeting that would have been held by the client under normal circumstances. The chairman was the member of the client organization whose brief was to develop the list of new concepts. He acted 'conventionally' – that is, he was an important contributor of ideas in contrast to the leader role advocated in this book. He described the objective of the meeting in terms of producing product ideas for future testing with consumers. He circulated a list of ideas which had been generated in an earlier meeting elsewhere in the company. He emphasized that he did not necessarily want technically sophisticated ideas. For the benefit of the proposed methodological research the meeting was tape-recorded. 41 ideas were collected, and the exercise lasted about three and a half hours. Most of the ideas were distinct from those on the document which had been circulated prior to the meeting.

In general, the participants felt it had been a 'good meeting'. The members of the ideas group were less approving, and all commented on the level of negativity and the way in which potentially good ideas had probably been lost because of the absence of procedures for recording and itemizing ideas in a way that could enable participants to see ideas at the time they were produced. The synectics-trained members would have preferred a chalk board or flipchart for displaying ideas.

Synectics meetings

The synectics meetings took place about a week after the first, formal session. Each meeting lasted about two and a half hours and had two separate metaphoric excursions in close succession. The second excursion in each case was considered unsatisfactory and heavy going by the participants. The entire synectics procedure was not well received. One of the less experienced participants felt that the leader had shown bias in favour of his fellow 'experts' in selecting ideas for further examination.

A small number of original ideas were produced which were later eliminated through lack of consumer approval.

Brainstorming session

The next meeting to be held was a brainstorming incorporating subroutines T.4.1, T.4.2 and T.4.4 with the 10 available members of the project team.

At this stage the participants had worked together in the normal meeting, and in one of the synectics sessions.

Approximately 400 idea statements were generated in an hour and a half of uninterrupted brainstorming. The group found it easy to postpone judgement and an extremely lighthearted atmosphere developed. The most experienced brainstormer present (who was not leading the group) commented afterwards that there was virtually no attempt at building on ideas of other people, the hilarity was excessive and nonconstructive, and the session had gone on at least half an hour too long. Another experienced brainstormer commented before evaluating the ideas that there seemed to be an 'above-average amount of rubbish' within the material produced.

Morphological analysis

Two different morphologies had been prepared, in order to accommodate technical and nontechnical members of the panel. The technical

Figure 8:5 Morphological analysis in a new-product concepts exercise

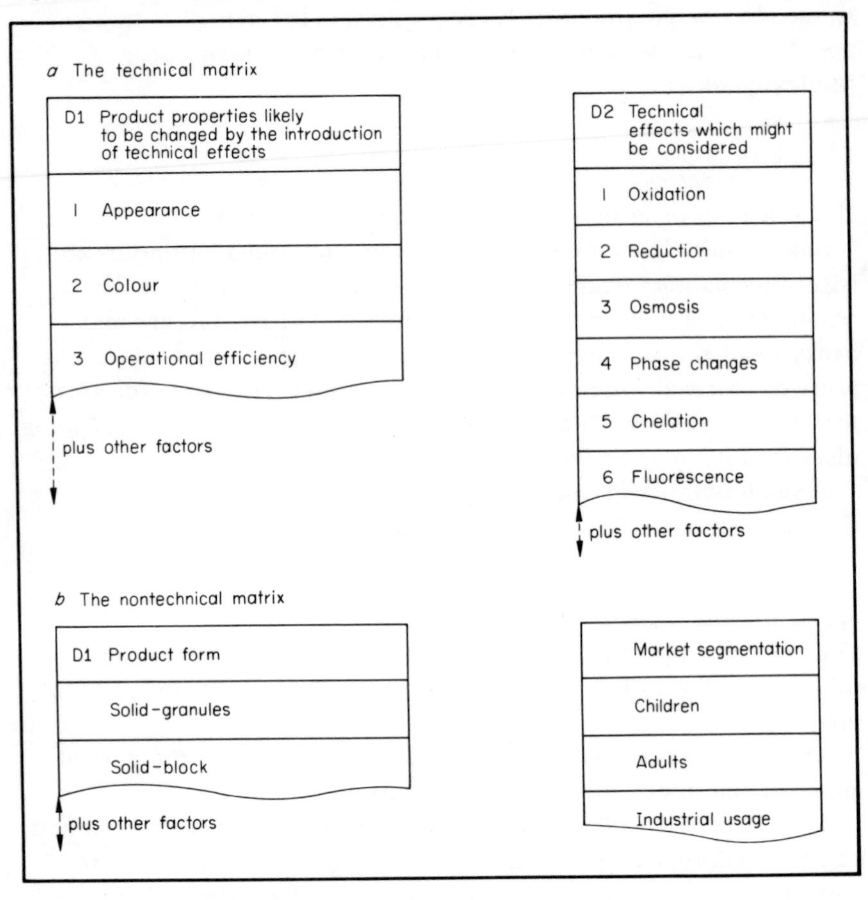

members shared matrix A in Figure 8:5 and the nontechnical ones matrix B. The first technical member was expected to return to the next meeting having considered and attempted to produce at least one idea for ways of influencing the product properties D1.1 (appearance) based on each of the technical effects D2.1, D2.2, and so on. If he could add to the list of effects, he should do so. In this way all of matrix A was distributed among the group members who had a technical background (about two-thirds of the entire panel). Matrix B was distributed in a similar way to the nontechnical members.

The results from the technology-based matrix were not suitable for the consumer-oriented immediate needs of the project. The participants felt that their ideas suggested possible new projects and that they should be given wider circulation throughout the laboratory. The nontechnical matrix did not help the members to produce ideas. They felt that it might have done at an earlier stage of the project, but having participated in three meetings, they found themselves blocked by previously generated concepts.

Other idea-generation exercises

In the course of the exercise several informal discussions took place. After the synectics session members of the ideas group addressed themselves to the apparent difficulty of holding two long excursions within a single synectics session. They experimented with a mixed synectics/brainstorming format, in which a large number of analogies were generated, and each example taken effectively as a random stimulus from which to develop new ideas related to the problem. They found that three such excursions could be held in an hour without the group becoming as tired as after the second excursion in the actual exercise.

Evaluation of the idea statements

The idea statements from all these exercises were collected together to make a list of about 500 concepts. The application of a simple screen as shown in Figure 3:5 reduced the list to approximately 150 concepts, and then to a short-list of 40 concepts. Approximately half of the total short-list were ideas that originated in the brainstorming session.

The concepts of the short-list were presented to panels of people thought likely to be consumers. The panels identified five products which had significantly greater appeal than the others. The results helped the direction of speculative research in which a project was initiated to establish the technical feasibility of one of the five winning concepts. The outright winner in the technical tests has been retested with 'market' concepts, and has repeatedly scored well. However, the assessment of technical feasibility in this case may have been incorrect and to date (1973) no prototype has been made which satisfies the concept implicit in the definitions tested.

8.4 CASE STUDY 3: COMMUNICATING A TECHNICAL EFFECT TO NONTECHNICAL PERSONNEL

In 1970 the ideas group worked with a manager who was developing a piece of technology which improved the performance of an important class of commercial compounds. He felt he had not been able to explain all the virtues to advertising and marketing people within the company, and defined his problem as 'how to communicate a technical effect to nontechnical personnel'.

A team from his own section and from the ideas group held two synectics sessions followed by a brainstorming at about one week intervals. A dozen ideas were produced from the synectics, and 100 from the brainstorming. A member of the project section clustered the ideas by an intuitive method (morphological analysis) into the categories shown in Figure 8:6.

As a first stage towards demonstrating the effect to nontechnical personnel it was decided to make a video representation. The ideas in categories 3, 4, 6, 7 and 8 were reexamined. From them a series of

Figure 8:6 Idea categories from a communications problem

1 Ways of reducing the time before the product advantage is noticed by the consumer.

2 Methods of better research/marketing interaction.

3 Visualizations involving filming, stereo, video, etc.

4 Nontechnical and evocative visualizations.

5 Nontechnical but mundane visualizations.

6 Key areas where the improvements would be most visible.

7 Existing laboratory tests which could be used to visualize the improvement.

8 Novel (wishful) demonstrations feasible in the laboratory.

9 Demonstrations that the consumer might be able to make for himself.

10 Changes to the product form or content.

11 Wishful ideas.

12 Promotional ideas based on the technical improvement.

demonstrations were filmed with a range of technical contents, from bald statements of technical measurements, right through to an analogy illustrating what the implications were in every day life (Figure 8:7).

A series of such visualizations was presented for discussion with the marketing personnel. As a consequence the technical implications were more easily conveyed to the nontechnical people. The technical implications which seemed highly significant to the marketing men were often those taken for granted and considered uninteresting or trivial by the technologists.

The original client considered that the brainstorming and synectics sessions had been highly successful, contributing to a valuable videotape. He felt that the ideas helped his insight into the problem, and influenced the subsequent treatment by his staff.

8.5 CASE STUDY 4: A FIVE-DAY TRAINING COURSE IN GROUP PROBLEM-SOLVING TECHNIQUES

The ideas section had had considerable experience in group problem-solving techniques by the end of 1971 and felt that a training course might serve to spread awareness of their procedures throughout the research division. Senior managers were asked to nominate staff who were interested and who intended to become involved in brainstorming or synectics sessions on a regular basis. Seven technical personnel were nominated, and attended a one-week course held in the idea group's conference room. A videotape recorder was available to help the teaching processes. The teaching methodology was strongly influenced by a belief that for this particular subject, an experimental approach was necessary. The participants would learn by doing rather than being lectured at.

Each member of the group brought along one or two problems in which he was involved, and for which he wanted fresh ideas. At the start of the first day, the group selected one and were asked to tackle it for half an hour in any way they liked. The procedures were monitored on closed-circuit television and video recording. This was followed by a post-mortem at which sequences were relayed to the group but without comment. There followed additional half-hour problem-solving sessions alternating with post-mortems. Based on the

Figure 8:7 *Representing a technical effect in nontechnical terms*

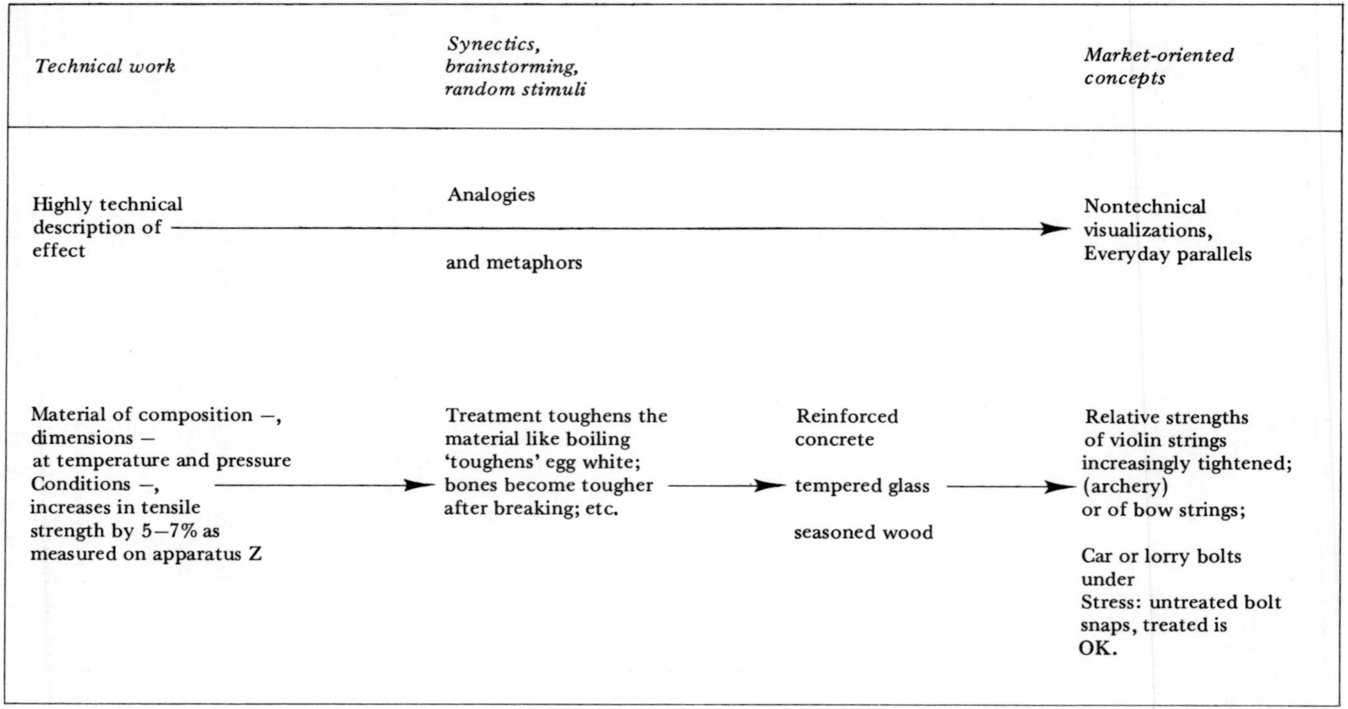

Technical work	*Synectics, brainstorming, random stimuli*		*Market-oriented concepts*
Highly technical description of effect →	Analogies and metaphors →		Nontechnical visualizations, Everyday parallels
Material of composition –, dimensions – at temperature and pressure Conditions –, increases in tensile strength by 5–7% as measured on apparatus Z →	Treatment toughens the material like boiling 'toughens' egg white; bones become tougher after breaking; etc. →	Reinforced concrete tempered glass seasoned wood →	Relative strengths of violin strings increasingly tightened; (archery) or of bow strings; Car or lorry bolts under Stress: untreated bolt snaps, treated is OK.

good and bad elements in the videotapes, the various concepts of synectics were introduced. After about a day and a half the group had learned and practised all the main elements of synectics without having it presented to them as a rigid set of procedures. It was hoped that the participants would go away and concentrate on problem-solving rather than worrying about the mechanics of problem-solving meetings.

The remainder of the second day was spent on practising the additional procedures involved in brainstorming, and illustrating the morphological method of structuring a problem. The relationship between a two-dimensional matrix and a binary relevance system was brought out.

The third and fourth days were devoted to tackling a real problem considered to be of considerable commercial interest to the division. The group tackled four aspects of the problem with experts from different parts of the company acting as clients. At the end of the series each client together with one or two members of the group spent about two hours evaluating the results of their session. This enabled participants to have an additional practical yardstick against which to measure the techniques about which they were learning.

Comments by the group members on the two days spent on this problem included:

1 Good idea to tackle a problem in depth in this way.
2 Four sessions on one problem was too much. Perhaps two problems should have been taken.
3 Four sessions in two days was too tiring.
4 A chance to tackle a problem completely divorced from our normal work would have been welcome.
5 The problem session's the real meat of this course.
6 It was useful to tackle a real problem.
7 Clients should all have been actively working on the problem.
8 It would be instructive to work in a group with vested interests in the problem, so as to show the effect of the techniques on personality clashes.

By the end of the week, the group members were running sessions for themselves, often combining the elements of brainstorming and synectics in a creative fashion. Frequently, use of a synectics excursion improved the variation and quality of ideas on a problem.

The overall view of the participants was a general conviction that parts of the technique, particularly the behavioural elements, are applicable in a wide variety of normal meetings. There was some concern however, that the words 'synectics' and 'brainstorming' might put people off, if introduced without adequate explanation.

Subsequent to the course, the material on the real problem was incorporated to some extent in projects in which the clients were involved. Two or three members who had been trained in the techniques returned with requests for further activities. This was the commonest development, for the participants did not proceed to implement the techniques consciously in their work situations. One or two, however, felt that they had become more positive in their attitudes towards ideas, particularly from subordinates.

8.6 NOTES ON CASE STUDIES 1–4

Case study 1

This is a good example of synectics procedures with emphasis on the metaphoric excursion. Students of synectics tend to worry about the level of skill needed to conduct such an apparently complex operation, and the difficulty the leader must experience in selecting good avenues to explore. In fact the technique including the excursion is extremely robust, and the selection made by the leader is rarely critical to the success or failure of the meeting. The rule of thumb to remember is: try to select *away* from the conventional concepts associated with the focal points of the problem. Thus, if, as here, the key point is measuring or identifying something in the context of an industrial system, the leader could choose as his excursion starting point, examples of measuring (or identifying) from the worlds of music, travel, ornithology – in fact anything divorced from engineering situations.

The same principle holds for the next stages. This sometimes results in a strong metaphoric thread running through the excursion. On occasions this thread is lost, but the group can still benefit, as the material generated becomes random stimuli (T.3.5) for further ideas. One frequently raised question about the excursion is, What if a different branch had been followed during the excursion? In this case, suppose the leader had chosen 'rats' instead of 'spiders'. Probably, similar types of ideas would have emerged, as the backgrounds of the participants make important contributions in each case. However, a different choice may result in losing the key idea, or in gaining a different but equally valuable one.

Case study 2

This study provides some comparative data about brainstorming, synectics and conventional meetings. However, the same group was present, so that the later sessions were probably influenced by the earlier ones. Although precise statistically substantiated observations are out of place, in this particular exercise the brainstorming session was undoubtedly the most valuable and conventional synectics was not as successful as an idea-generation procedure. In fact, the synectics procedures used unmodified are more suited to obtaining possible solutions to problems than for generating lists of ideas. Furthermore, some of the participants were clearly not happy about the operating methods of synectics (which suggests that more time should have been spent preparing them for the exercise). Also, the attempt to run two excursions might be questioned. After one excursion, there is a perceptible change in the atmosphere and behaviour and a sort of trough which must be escaped from, before any further highly speculative excursion should be considered.

The outcome of the exercise is rather poignant. From 500 ideas, a short-list of 40 resulted giving five winners, out of which one has led to a new research project, with the potentially most valuable idea still not being exploited.

Case study 3

A very common class of problem – 'how to communicate . . .' The strategy adopted appears successful. The alternative approach is to argue that the sphere of influence of a communication problem encloses the two community subgroups. In this case, perhaps the problem could best have been tackled by a group containing both R and D and marketing personnel (and, if possible, some of the people who would actually pay to use the product).

The wide range of ideas produced by the techniques could not be evaluated by the research group alone. This was demonstrated by the reactions of the marketeers, who had quite distinct ideas about what could be relevant to a marketing strategy. (So, once again, a mixed group would have been preferable.)

The existence of such a problem is further evidence of the growing market orientation of technical managers in product or process environments.

Case study 4

An attempt to learn by doing. On one level the course was successful (some people came back to the ideas group later with fresh problems). The apparent lack of application of the techniques by the actual participants is more disturbing. Brainstorming (and even more so, synectics) retains an element of mystique which can deter people from trying it out for themselves. This point should be strongly stressed during training.

The participants were nominated, not the best way to obtain commitment (see Case Study 8) although it did not seem to matter in this case.

In practice interest in group creativity techniques seems to arise within a subunit of a company, perhaps through a technical director or marketing manager. In this sort of situation the training course should be designed around the heads of that subunit, and its participants should come from several levels of management within its hierarchy.

However, the strength of groups in problem-solving often stems from the bringing together of different points of view, so the course will be more valuable if problems are tackled which are interface ones (that is, involving personnel from other divisions).

Chapter 9

Case Studies Initiated by Various In-company Service Divisions

Service departments have been among the major in-company initiators of group problem-solving exercises. In this chapter examples are given from five different firms. Each case study concerns a different part of the firm: an OR section, a new ventures group, a training department, a long-range planning group and a market research unit.

Most of the work described was conducted during the period 1971–72 and none of it before 1965.

9.1 CASE STUDY 5: A SYSTEM FOR ACCELERATING INNOVATION DEVELOPED BY AN OR *GROUP WITHIN A DEVELOPMENT UNIT OF A CONSUMER-GOODS ORGANIZATION*

As part of its longer-term policy, the OR group within a consumer-goods organization had been developing an interest in aids to innovation over the period 1969–73. The first experiments involved one manager in scanning the aids to creativity and, in particular, group methods such as brainstorming and synectics. He found brainstorming useful in a variety of development problems in which the OR group were involved, on a contract research basis, with the production unit of the company.

He was initially less convinced of the value of synectics, commenting later that although everyone was enthusiastic it was hard to identify any ideas which later developed into new products or processes. He concluded that the technique might have been oversold and that he had helped produce a lot of elegant and creative ideas that were in general outside the control of the client and not easily implemented.

He eventually opted for adoption of a variety of techniques, some analytical and some creative with the overall objective of making the innovation process more rapid, certain and profitable. He has called his system one for accelerating innovation, and bases it on four stages of problem-solving: analysis, synthesis, collation, evaluation.

Potential problem analysis

The members of the OR group have developed a method of anticipating problems in process-development exercises. In one example they were able to identify how a change from pilot-plant conditions to full-scale production would result in considerable additional hazards in handling one particular material. As a result of the analysis contingency plans were initiated during the development stages to eliminate the hazard.

The key stage in the analysis was a reverse brainstorming, in which the question was asked, 'What might possibly go wrong with the full-scale process?' Among the ideas was 'the material might be spilled and washed down the drains'. Examination revealed that contingency plans were needed to prevent spillage being washed away in this fashion as serious blockages would almost certainly occur.

Synectics experience

Although initial efforts were unfavourable, the group persevered with synectics and eventually introduced the technique into training courses for middle managers. To date their most striking success arose from a session with children of company personnel on the topic of inventing a new food for children. The session was conducted by a skilled leader but the children were given a minimum of operational instructions beyond being encouraged to speculate. The expert (who had the project brief of developing the product) was also present. The children suggested two ideas which the expert was able to convert into technically feasible and original concepts, and which were patented. Based on the argument that the children 'only' provided the stimulus which enabled the technical expert to create and validate the item, he alone was named as inventor. The products eventually reached the market-place in 1973.

Overall 'accelerated innovation' system

The group handles problems in a service capacity at a rate of about 30 a year. Its input varies from assistance at corporate level down to helping a manager overcome specific sub-problems within a project. The entire middle management within one large division of the company has been initiated into the principles and practices of accelerated innovation. Many of the aids described in Part One are included in the system (Figure 9:1), some under different titles. The aids are seen as tactics within the total problem-solving system which give reinforcements to the different stages of analysis, synthesis, collation and evaluation.

Concept challenge is a form of boundary examination (T.3.6); lateral thinking is Dr Edward de Bono's term for various methods for facilitating redefinitional insights including random juxtaposition (nonlogical stimuli T.3.5); hypothetical situation is a rather unstructured forecasting procedure as in scenario building (both described

Figure 9:1 Tactics employed in a total system for accelerated innovation

Analysis	*Synthesis*	*Collation*	*Evaluation*
Concept challenge	Synectics plus excursions	Cross-examination of expert in session (criticality testing)	Screening procedures; weighting
Potential problem identification (brainstorming)			
Checklist methods	Lateral thinking (random juxta-position)	Clear simple reporting	Establishment of critical test steps
Lateral thinking	Role playing	Idea development (scenario) building	Concept testing
Cross-examination	Hypothetical situation		Research planning diagrams

in textbooks on technological forecasting); criticality testing is based on establishing actions and agents in each stage during progression of an idea.

9.2 CASE STUDY 6: A SEARCH FOR NEW BUSINESS OPPORTUNITIES

A European organization with interests in the service industries set up a small new-business group in 1972. A director was appointed who had had several years' experience as a senior marketing executive in an analogous industry with a different company.

The group established financial and marketing criteria for potential new businesses, in conjunction with feedback from the company board. Suggestions for new opportunities were collected through conventional routes (in-company discussions, etc.), and a programme of idea-generation sessions was to be initiated by the new-business manager, who had been exposed to synectics and brainstorming in his previous company.

First idea-generation meeting

The first meeting was held informally in the manager's office. He led the session himself with the declared intention of permitting a wide-ranging discussion which would test out the techniques and perhaps also generate some good ideas. Group composition is shown in Figure 9:2. Several problems were listed and one selected as the main topic for the day's activities. New ways of looking at this problem were noted (19 in all), and these were clustered in four interrelated areas. This was followed by a brainstorming ('how do we create new products or new opportunities to satisfy these identified areas'). Nearly 50 ideas were obtained in just under half an hour. The wildest idea from the brainstorming was taken as the starting point for a synectics excursion which included several different stages. The material from the final stage was related back to the problem and three possible solutions obtained.

In retrospect the group decided that the techniques had helped them think of new ideas and that their creativity could be reinforced by calling in a consultant to lead the subsequent meetings.

Figure 9:2 *Summary of three ideas meetings for new business opportunities*

Meeting number	*Venue*	*Participants*	*Format*	*Perceived value and outcome*
1	NBM's office	NBM, S, PS, ANBM	Informal 'ideas' meeting about 3 hours long	Thought to be highly successful by group, no implementation of ideas
2	Conference room in hotel	C, NBM, PS, ANBM, O	Formal – about 3 hours long	Thought to be very poor; one idea is being examined
3	Conference room in hotel	C, MM, NBM, PS, ANBM, AC	Formal – about 4½ hours including working lunch	Improvement over (2) but not as good as (1). MM intended to pursue ideas further

KEY:

NBM	New business manager
S	Secretary (female) to NBM
PS	Psychologist (female)
ANBM	Assistant to NBM
O	Outsider (creative professional man)
C	Consultant
MM	Marketing Manager
AC	Assistant to C (female)
—	Underlined person acts as group leader
═	Underlined person acts as client or expert (none in meeting 1 but two in meeting 3)

Second idea-generation meeting

The second meeting was arranged jointly by the new-business manager (the client) and an outside consultant who was to act as group leader. The consultant had been provided with a list of problems that the company considered important. They agreed a longer-term plan whereby the group would develop skills and eventually become independent of the consultant. Approximately one month after the first meeting a second took place under more formal circumstances (Figure 9:2). The ideas team first took an icebreaking lunch for the two participants from outside the company to become acquainted with the other members of the group. After lunch the team moved to a small conference room equipped with flip-charts and easy chairs.

The format was: an orientation session by the leader, a period of redefinitions, selection of the most promising redefinitions, collection of ideas based on a number of redefinitions selected by the client, and extension of a small number of ideas again selected by the client. To this stage the group had produced concepts of a rather mundane nature, although the client indicated that one or two ideas had suggested actions which he could initiate after the meeting. The leader then encouraged a short period of speculative thinking introduced by a one-stage synectics excursion, which did most appreciably help the group. During the excursion the group tried to build a collective image based on an analogy to the problem. On returning to the problem the ideas that were obtained were similar to those which had been produced earlier. The session concluded with a brainstorming (about 60 ideas in 10 minutes) to obtain a list of possible trade names for the enterprise that had been developed during the exercise. A summary report was drawn up immediately by the consultant and the new-business manager's assistant and circulated to the members.

After the meeting, the company personnel expressed considerable dissatisfaction. They felt the meeting was 'a lot worse' than the first one. In his own notes the consultant had observed that there had seemed little need for structured techniques; the lunch had been 'over-adequate at loosening up the group'; the most interesting idea had emerged almost immediately after the start of the meeting; and thereafter the members had found it difficult to act as a task-oriented unit.

During a telephone discussion between manager and consultant these views were exchanged. It emerged that one of the ideas (the early one) was being actively followed up. The manager repeated his wishes that his people 'wanted to be worked harder' if they decided to hold another meeting. This took place about two months after the second meeting.

Third idea-generation activity

The new-business manager, in a telephone discussion with the consultant agreed to try another session to see if it could be an improvement over the previous one. The consultant emphasized the value that could be gained from group members who were outside the new-business manager's division, and it was agreed that two new members, both experienced in idea-generation and group problem-solving procedures, should be introduced. The consultant nominated his secretary, and an advertising executive known to both parties from earlier experience.

The actual idea-generation meeting was arranged to take place as quickly as possible, but the consultant visited the new-business manager a week before the meeting to clarify aspects such as its main objectives, composition of the group, and the specific problems to be tackled. At that time the consultant and the new-business manager reexamined the lists of redefinitions obtained in the earlier meetings. They tried to establish the types of ideas which might emerge and how these ideas would be developed. The most suitable problems for the next meeting proved to be ones which required that a colleague of the new-business manager, the marketing manager, should act as client. It had already been agreed that the marketing manager should be included in the group. The consultant expressed some concern about 'volunteering' a client and was additionally perturbed when the new-business manager requested that, for confidentiality reasons, the advertising executive (on whom they had originally agreed) be excluded from the meeting.

Thus the group for the actual meeting was made up of a marketing man as client, the outside consultant as leader, the new-business manager, two of his staff members, and a secretary who was a skilled synectics practitioner from the consultant organization. The meeting took place in yet another venue, this time a hotel conference room. A light lunch was provided, and the meeting arranged to run from

11 am until the group had exhausted the topic. In fact it was discovered that the two senior company executives had to leave early, so that it was agreed to conclude the meeting at the time when they left.

The format was basically the same as that of the previous meeting – a synectics session including a period of itemization of responses, and an excursion. It concluded with a short brainstorming session.

The client (the marketing manager) appeared to be rather neutral towards the procedure, and did not indicate any enthusiasm towards any ideas produced. The new-business manager demonstrated a high level of individual creativity, but the individuals present found it difficult to act as a cooperative group in idea development or improvement.

After the meeting the marketing manager requested a comprehensive report and indicated that he would like his own managers to take part in a subsequent meeting. The new-business manager and the consultant were less happy about the session, and it was agreed shortly afterwards that the company would continue with idea-generation activities but without the consultant.

9.3 CASE STUDY 7: A TRAINING DEPARTMENT INTRODUCING BRAINSTORMING AS AN INTEGRATING DEVICE AT THE START OF A TRAINING COURSE

A well-known financial institution in the UK holds regular courses for its managers, who develop skills through working together in small groups on real problems. It had been noted by the training manager that for the first day or so a lot of time was spent wastefully as the trainees became accustomed to each other. He discovered that this period could be reduced after he introduced brainstorming at the start of the course.

Brainstorming exercise

A commercially available slide and tape package was used. This introduces the concepts of close- and open-ended problems (defined as having a logically correct, and having no logically correct answer, respectively). Series of puzzles of both types are presented, including an exercise near the beginning of the session and another similar one towards the end when the group has warmed up. In general the more relaxed mood at the end, and an understanding of the value of intuitive, apparently irrelevant, ideas, lead to a higher score in the second test. This is extended to explain the principles of (Osborn) brainstorming. An actual group is heard brainstorming, and then the participants are invited to join in with ideas. In the final stages, the participants brainstorm their own problem.

On the first occasion that he used the package, the trainer included a real marketing problem and supplied the results to the marketing director of the company.

Consequences of the brainstorming

As indicated, after brainstorming, the group more rapidly reached cohesive and task-oriented attitudes. An unexpected bonus to the exercise was to develop, however. A summary of the ideas was submitted to the marketing director for information. He was surprised at the apparent ignorance of the trainees on matters of marketing intelligence and company policy which he felt they should know. As a result he attended subsequent courses and introduced a regular bulletin on matters of marketing importance.

The managers on later courses became more sophisticated in evaluating the ideas from the brainstorming, and in one instance a concept thus derived led to modified recruitment advertising on the part of the company.

9.4 *CASE STUDY 8: AN EXERCISE TO GENERATE NEW BUSINESS IDEAS WITHIN AN ENGINEERING CONGLOMERATE*

A large engineering conglomerate has a research and development laboratory which is mainly concerned with the improvement and maintenance of existing product lines. A new-activities group (NA group) was set up to look for opportunities of a more revolutionary kind, while still exploiting the company's engineering and process skills. Ideas for new products traditionally come from the company's technical intelligence service, licence and patent searches, and trade contacts. In addition each member of the NA group monitored an area within the mainstream interests of the company, either one being developed at present or one which might become important in a foreseeable time scale.

The technical director of the main R and D laboratory enlisted the aid of the NA group in an exercise of a more open-ended nature, which was to involve a major proportion of the engineers and other technologists within his department.

Idea-generation activities

Approximately 100 technical personnel took part in the exercise, which initially lasted for two days. The participants had been instructed to attend via their senior managers. The sessions were introduced by the technical director who outlined the importance of the exercise to the diversification plans of the entire group. He also explained the need for producing ideas outside the confines of their existing business and pointed out that they should give speculative concepts a fair trial in the next two days.

The personnel were divided into groups of approximately eight people. At the end of the exercise a total of about 250 ideas had been produced and discussed, each with a record of its origin.

A summary of the results was drawn up by the NA group and circulated to all participants, who then took part in an evaluation session, again in groups of eight, to consider a short-list of about 30 ideas. Wherever possible the originator of an idea was included in the group evaluating and developing it.

After this stage about 10 ideas had satisfied corporate and technical feasibility, and financial criteria. The follow-up work is to be left to the originators of the ideas. If any of these are able to establish an acceptable case for progressing the idea, resources and capital will be provided. It is the intention of the company to include the man who had the original idea in the venture team if he retains his interest and enthusiasm for the project.

The NA group felt, in reviewing the exercise, that almost all the suggestions had been very close to existing businesses. They noted that two or three members of most of the ideas groups had been pessimistic and rather uncooperative, possibly having an adverse effect on the quality and quantity of the ideas produced.

9.5 CASE STUDY 9: INTEGRATION OF IDEA-GENERATION AND GROUP BEHAVIOURAL EXERCISES BY A UNIT WITHIN A MARKET RESEARCH ORGANIZATION

One European market research company has extended the service it can offer to its customers by acquiring skills in structured idea-generation and problem-solving techniques. A small creativity group was set up inside the company, members being selected through appraisal interviews with emphasis on creative potential.

In its earliest meetings the group tackled problems with synectics procedures. The routines to overcome negativity towards ideas were followed carefully, but an impression was left that basic attitudes remained unchanged, while spontaneous expressions of dislike were being disguised in a series of ritualistic responses.

The group hired the services of a consultancy specializing in encounter techniques developed from work at the Esalen Institute in California. A 3-day training course was arranged to integrate idea-generation procedures with improvements in group behaviour.

The format of the course was a sequence of behavioural and idea-generation exercises on genuine company briefs, interacting as shown in Figure 9:3.

Behavioural exercises

The behavioural exercises attempted to cultivate spontaneity of expression, and an appreciation of the way in which each person is limited by others in the group and how he in turn limits those surrounding him. The behavioural implications of the exercises overlapped in a way that is not shown in Figure 9:3. Typical exercises included the following.

A space-perception exercise. Each participant created a personal zone, building it with the few pieces of domestic furniture available. The members took it in turn to visit other people's 'territories', but without attempts at rationalizations of their feelings.

In an exercise in group sensitivity, the participants stood in a circle and one of them started a gesture which was taken up and transmitted by the person next to him. This was repeated around the circle, with considerable distortion. A similar exercise in transmission of rhythm was displayed. In an exercise in personal risk, one member stood, eyes closed, in the middle of a circle, close enough to prevent

Figure 9:3 A system of sequential idea-generation and behavioural exercises for small groups

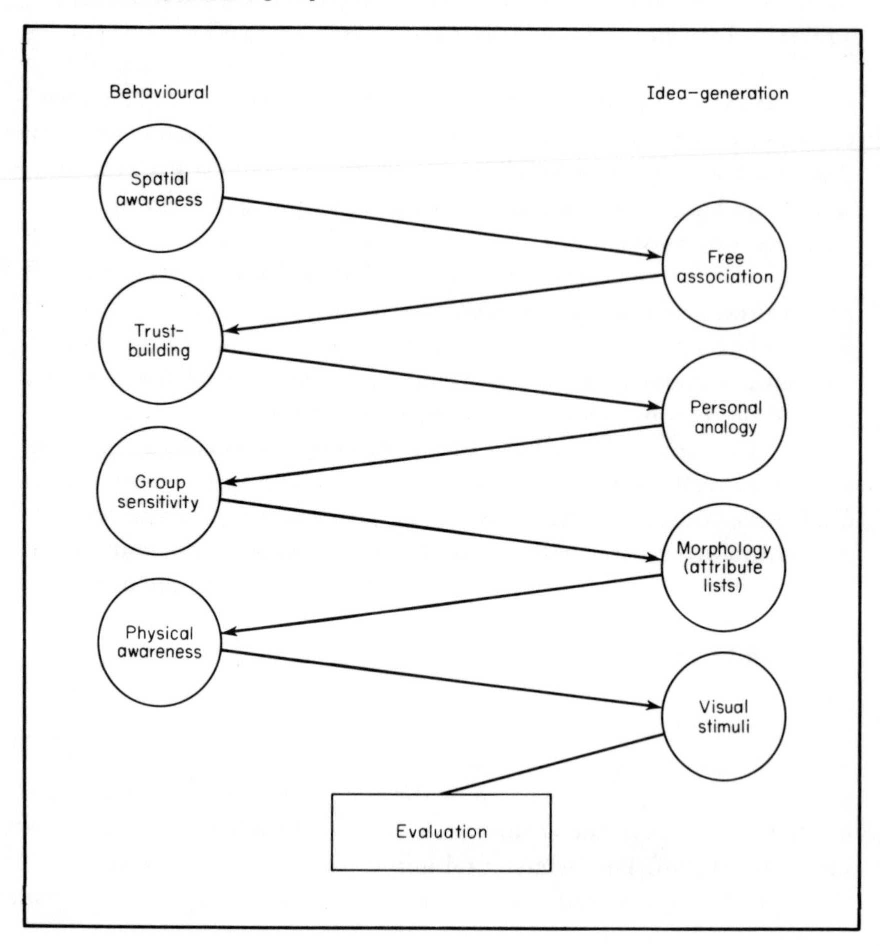

him falling. He allows himself to fall towards the group and was pushed gently about the circle. As confidence grew he took greater risks, and fell across a wider arc.

The physical awareness exercise is an encouragement for people to become more aware of each other through looking and touching partners. A silent routine was followed by an expression of feelings and perceptions gained, but in which interpretive discussion was discouraged.

Idea-generation techniques
Each of the techniques (shown in Figure 9:3) helped the group to achieve 'distance' from the problem and then to return to it with fresh insights. In the free association exercise, the members took a key word from the problem definition and in turn built up a sequence of words freely associated with the one before it. The final words were taken as starting points for new ideas.

In the personal analogy exercise, the group members tried to identify with some aspect of the problem ('what does it *feel* like to be a toothpaste?') Insights about new physical structures of inanimate objects can be obtained in this way.

The morphology exercise was linked to Osborn's idea-spurring questions. A product matrix was set up with the dimensions of form, function and context. For each element in each dimension, five operations were considered: add, multiply, divide, subtract, reverse. A typical matrix would look like the one in Figure 9:4. The circled combination might suggest ideas based on apples as the immediate solution. Thinking of a divided product suggests individual pieces of chewing gum; reversing one's thoughts from edible to nonedible materials may spark off ideas of toothpicks or cleaning pads.

In the projection technique a series of out-of-focus slides was projected in front of the group, whose members attempted to see

Figure 9:4 Typical matrix for generating new-product ideas for a new tooth cleaner

Dimensions	
Form	Paste, gel, powder, cream, (solid,) etc.
Function	Polish, (protect,) clean, whiten, purify, etc.
Context	Bathroom, travelling, (in work,) morning, evening, etc.
Users	Children, (all people,) animals, etc.

Check each combination for opportunities of adding, multiplying, dividing, subtracting, reversing.

significance in terms of the problem. Over 100 ideas were obtained for one problem by this technique alone.

Evaluation stage
Emphasis was given to the differing psychological needs for effective idea generation and evaluation. In the first instance attempts were made to create an informal atmosphere. The surroundings were relaxed, and people were encouraged to sit on the floor, take off their jackets, or do anything else which made them feel at home. During the evaluation stage, however, the group was moved into a formal situation seated around a table.

Consequences of the exercise
Some time after returning to their everyday problems, the group members decided that the exercise had helped improve their interpersonal behaviour. They continued to run the idea-generation sessions with increased awareness of the importance of generating and elaborating ideas in discrete stages. They may repeat the training exercise if this becomes necessary, although new members are currently introduced into the group without the behavioural training.

9.6 NOTES ON CASE STUDIES 5–9

In each case the team or individual introducing an idea-generating problem-solving technique was acting in a service capacity. The problems therefore fall outside its sphere of influence and identifying and redirecting key personnel become important factors (see Section 1.4). This was done more deliberately in Case Study 8, with feedback to idea originators and involving them wherever possible. In some cases there might be other groups whose participation would have altered the types of idea produced – for example, consumers in Case Study 6, marketing personnel in Case Study 8.

The cases represent sensible attempts to initiate creative activities in groups without a great deal of prior consultation with experienced practitioners. The results should be encouraging to other groups who might have refrained from trying out group techniques, because of lack of experience. An informed adviser should help to improve on the methodology in subsequent experiments, but there is no guarantee that this will lead to immediately recognizable results (see Case Study 6).

Case study 5
The group had developed according to the principles and practice of creative analysis, introducing and modifying various techniques and their subroutines. Even more attention to the efforts needed to get ideas accepted and to the concept of the true agent or client might have overcome some of the problems experienced with using synectics. Professional help might also have been valuable at that stage.

Case study 6
At first these examples seem to indicate that the group would have been better off if it had continued to develop its expertise without outside interference from creativity consultants. There are complexities which make such an instant judgement doubtful, however. The first session was undoubtedly the least formal, and the one which had the greatest impact in convincing the participants of the value of aids to creativity. The second session, probably the most structured and formal, did lead to implementation of one of the concepts generated. The client and consultant were evaluating the meeting from different viewpoints – the former as a creativity-boosting device, the latter probably as a means of identifying actionable ideas. In the third session, better communication had been established, and a more acceptable meeting took place as a consequence. Their different points of view should have been resolved, perhaps by the consultant in pre-meeting consultation.

Case study 7
This is a neat example of a rather unusual reason for introducing brainstorming, but one which might be copied by other training groups. In addition, the concentration on a real problem accidentally identified the agent who was actively concerned to encourage work in the area (the marketing director). As a direct consequence of this involvement the ideas were given a very good opportunity of being implemented. The feedback from him led to increased sophistication and improvement in possible solutions in later exercises.

Case study 8
The new-activities group observed that the ideas were rather close to existing products and projects. Two factors contributed to this: the composition of the ideas groups was rather homogeneous; the

preliminary instructions did not emphasize adequately that evaluation should be separated from idealism. In addition the groups were 'volunteered' and contained some dissidents who were negatively disposed to new ideas. Nevertheless, this must be judged a good and successful exercise. The attempts to involve the originators in progressing ideas are particularly commendable and should strengthen the viability of any venture groups which emerge.

It will be possible to improve in subsequent exercises – the negative people can be excluded from the groups and a serious effort to postpone judgement during the evaluation stage leads to a wider-ranging set of concepts. (Two hundred and fifty ideas could be produced by a single group in about an hour, after a few hours of warm-up exercises.)

Case study 9

The exercise represents a serious and commendable attempt at marrying encounter-type experiences with structured aids to creativity. Groups in other work environments could well experiment in a similar fashion. However, an appreciation of the value of such experiential techniques cannot be gained through case studies. (See Appendix 2 for UK practitioners.) The origins of the idea-generation sessions can be traced to synectics (T.5.5), nonlogical stimuli (T.3.5), reversals (T.3.7), and the restructuring techniques (T.1.1), (T.1.3).

Chapter 10

Using Consumers to Generate New-product Ideas

10.1 INTRODUCTION

Most manufacturers involve consumers in the invention and development of new-product ideas but the involvement is often indirect – for example, by modifying a concept as a result of market research interviews and questionnaires – in the consumer goods area. A more recent trend is to bring together the new-product team members and the consumers at the earliest stage possible in the project. The case studies in this chapter describe experiences in the UK, America and continental Europe since 1970 and are mostly pertinent to the consumer-goods industries.

10.2 CASE STUDY 10: NOP EXPERIENCE IN USING CONSUMERS TO GENERATE NEW-PRODUCT IDEAS

One of the earlier attempts in the UK to use consumers to generate new-product ideas was by Mr Peter Sampson of National Opinion Polls Ltd. Describing this work, Sampson (1970) compared the results obtained from:

1 Conventional group discussions.

2 'Brainstorming' groups.
3 Groups using synectics.

Conventional and brainstorming groups inventing new food products for children

The conventional group discussion involved eight housewives, all with young children, from social classes C1 and C2. The topic was new food and drink products for children. The ideas tended to be variations on existing products, with emphasis on changes in flavour and packaging. The results appeared to have little of value or originality when examined subsequently by the professional researchers.

The brainstorming group (which tackled the same problem) had been assembled with different underlying principles. There was a wider range of ages from teenagers to a grandparent, and social class ranged from B to C2. Some of the members had no direct or immediate interest in children. Members of the group had already shown above-average ability to generate answers in an open-ended test ('how many uses can you think of for a housebrick?').

In the first part of the meeting, background information was provided about children's food and drinks. This was followed by an idea-generation stage during which the group was subdivided. Each subgroup had to invent and develop the idea for a product, covering as many aspects as possible including name and price.

In the final (idea-development) stage, a nominee from each group presented the product to the entire panel arbitrarily divided into members role-playing as 'parents' and 'children'.

In his evaluation of the exercise Sampson concluded that the brainstorming approach had succeeded better in facilitating creative thought: the results were altogether more imaginative and he attributed this to the informal atmosphere and the ease whereby divergent ideas could be produced as a result of the brainstorming structure.

Synectics experiments

Two groups were assembled according to principles described by W. J. J. Gordon in his book, *Synectics* (1961). The participants had diverse backgrounds, appeared to be above-average in intelligence (assessed by job and education) and showed a capacity for divergent thinking. The format of the meeting put strong emphasis on a metaphoric excursion. The first group was an all male one, with five idea-generators and two noncontributing leaders. It examined the task of designing a new domestic appliance. The leaders were impressed by the originality of the concepts generated, but the groups never succeeded in converging towards a meaningful solution. It was concluded that the problem might be too complex for the technique.

The second group again had two 'moderators' (leaders) and five nonspecialists, two of whom were female. The problem was to invent a completely new educational toy or game suitable for children of unspecified age. The group became completely involved in the project and developed a product on the concept of water passing through tubes, sluice gates, etc. Nonparticipants observing the exercise did not share the enthusiasm of the group about the value of the concept.

Sampson summed up his experiments as follows:

> The creativity-spurring techniques helped to express new product ideas in such a context that they can be taken to a logical stage of processing. Within the time-span of a few hours it would be more likely that such a partial solution would emerge rather than a complete solution. Notwithstanding certain constraints regarding the type of problem which might be tackled, the new techniques seemed to offer a promising alternative to conventional group discussions for problems that require inventiveness.

10.3 CASE STUDY 11: AN EXERCISE IN COMMUNICATIONS BETWEEN TECHNOLOGISTS AND CONSUMERS

A group of food technologists had been working on a modification to a popular ingredient found in various foodstuffs. Their modified products would have better storage properties and would be cheaper to produce. The main market for the technology had already been developed but there was interest in examining additional potential uses for the material. An informal synectics session was arranged which brought together the project team with potential users of the new products, recruited from wives and girlfriends of the company personnel involved in the project.

The leader explained to the group, and particularly to the housewives who had never participated in synectics sessions, that this was a form of group discussion. Every effort would be made to help the housewives understand what the scientists were trying to do in nontechnical terms. To this end, he, as leader, would act as a neutral chairman whose job would be to ensure that every idea was given a fair chance.

One of the food technologists acted as the client, explaining how their new material was considered by nutritionists to be as good as the natural material and superior in terms of preservation properties.

The housewives showed considerable suspicion regarding the motives both of the technologists and of their company, and found great difficulty in accepting a mutually acceptable objective for the meeting. The client originally defined the problem as: 'How to find new products incorporating X'.

The housewives made it quite clear that they did not particularly want to have X in any new product. When the leader asked the client to redefine the problem, to take into account the concern of the housewives, he suggested: 'How to sell more of X'.

In spite of all attempts to the contrary, the group polarized into the two subgroups of technologists and housewives. The former from time to time reiterated that the product was as nutritious, or as tasty, or of equally acceptable texture, as any natural material. On the other side, the housewives repeated that the material was not natural and it might be extremely difficult to predict what unexpected undesirable attributes it might possess.

Towards the end of the meeting, the group did generate some new ideas using a sort of brainstorming. On examination, however, very little of value seemed to have emerged from the afternoon. Most members of the group thought that the activity had been a waste of time, although the leader (who was divorced from the project) felt that he could see the reasons for the difficulty.

Within six months the particular project was abandoned.

10.4 CASE STUDY 12: CREATIVITY-TESTING OF HOUSEWIVES TO AID SELECTION OF IDEA-GENERATION GROUPS

In 1971 a researcher within a market research organization applied himself to the problem of how to find consumers who would help to generate new ideas and would also make more meaningful contributions to interviews or group discussions. In the first instance, he was dealing with products bought and used mainly by housewives, so he began with a list of 50 housewives who had taken part in group discussions organized previously by the company. These 50 were themselves a short-list thought likely by their interviewers to be responsive in synectics sessions. The numbers were further reduced after a vocabulary test, on the principle that those people with the lowest scores were probably less able to communicate well in group activities. Those who passed the test were given two additional tests. The first of these was in five subsections, and in each of these the subject had to give uses for an everyday object with which she was familiar in the home – such as salt, a duster, a needle, a box of matches or milk. (These were similar to but not the actual words used.) Each housewife was given five minutes for each subsection. In a second test of five-minute duration each housewife was asked to doodle starting from a circle. The test paper was made up of a series of circles to which could be added doodles as the subject pleased. For each test, scores were evaluated by the total number of ideas produced, and the rareness of response ('rareness' is equivalent to infrequency of the response when results from all tests are compared) with respect to other housewives. Based on the tests, the housewives were classified into three clusters (high, medium and low scoring). Brainstorming sessions were held with the cluster which had the highest average scores on the test and also with the cluster with the medium scores.

In the first such experiments, the high-scoring group was dominated by a highly articulate housewife who produced what the organizer described as a series of 'When I was in Normandy on holiday we had . . .' type of ideas.

In contrast to the first group, the second was more cooperative, involved and seemed to produce more original ideas. This group seemed in general rather less educated than the former. As a result of these and later experiences, the experimenter concluded that creativity tests alone could not be considered adequate for separating people into groups for idea-generation activities.

As a further control, two other groups made up of professional market research personnel tackled the same problem. A comparison of the results of the four groups suggested that the professionals were not able to identify completely with the problems of the consumers.

10.5 CASE STUDY 13: 'EXTENDED CREATIVITY GROUPS' FOR NEW-PRODUCT DEVELOPMENT

The Gene Reilly organization (New York, USA) has been experimenting with methods for new-product development which involve bringing together groups of consumers and company personnel. An important aspect of the methodology is application of synectics principles to facilitate and encapsulate the development process into an intensive exercise lasting about two days, during which time product ideas are produced, modified and evaluated. Reilly has called his working unit an 'extended creativity group' or ECG.

Selection of participants in an ECG

An ECG comprises 'providers' from the company and 'needers' from potential consumers. Three to five personnel make up the providers, carefully selected to include those people who will have key decision-making roles at a later date within the project. One of these members is identified as being most closely related to the problem and is usually in middle or top management. He will act as the spokesman within the group as he is the one who will be asked to translate ideas into action. Company participants have included presidents, vice-presidents of marketing, product and brand managers, group marketing managers, market researchers, research and development personnel, and advertising agency representatives who might later have to provide support strategies. The need group can be made up of eight to ten people presumed to be representative of the target population who will buy the product. Two or three of these have been selected from a panel of about 600 people available to the company because they have had experience with synectics problem-solving methods. The experience may have come from sessions with other private firms or with the Reilly organization, but providers are never included twice with the same client or with the same type of problem.

Additional members of the ECG provided by the Reilly organization with knowledge of group behaviour act as leaders and generally try to reinforce good interpersonal relations. They also complete a report on meetings in a form that will be understandable and actionable by the client firm.

Operation of an ECG

Before the formation of an ECG there is a considerable amount of preplanning during which the methodology is described in detail to the client, and his needs and objectives are carefully worked out.

Functioning of an ECG based on synectics, has several aspects which distinguish it from conventional meeting procedures. The first is the differentiation between the role of the leader who remains a neutral-status person not contributing to the problem-solving and client roles. This new type of leader concentrates on the protection of initially weak ideas and on helping them survive. In particular, a formalized way of doing this, called *itemized response* (see Appendix 1) obliges participants to state three things they like about an idea before they say what they dislike about it. This is seen as having a unique advantage of 'keeping in the game people who might otherwise drop out the moment the going got rough' (Gene Reilly).

In addition analogy and metaphor are used as a means of making problem-solving more efficient and enjoyable. The group, which can include up to 15 people, may work together or may split into smaller groups for part of the time.

10.6 NOTES ON CASE STUDIES 10–13

The case studies throw some light on the problem of selecting non-specialist participants for idea-generation sessions. Case Studies 10 and 11 reinforce the view that creativity tests alone cannot be taken as the single guiding principle for selection. At the present state of knowledge the American method commends itself: competence in group meetings can be established by performance in earlier group meetings.

Nevertheless, the techniques seemed to operate satisfactorily even with crude selection methods. The process of bringing together specialists and nonspecialists can have benefits other than production of new product ideas. In Case Study 11 the result was increased perception of the real needs of the consumers by the food technologists.

Similar methods have been described with groups of children with ages from seven upwards. One case study leading to the invention and patenting of a new toothpaste can be found in Prince (1970). The children were encouraged to use the synectics processes during the meeting. Similar claims have also been made for recent innovations both in ice-cream and confectionery products in the UK.

Chapter 11

Miscellaneous Brainstorming Activities

11.1 INTRODUCTION

Brainstorming, more than most of the techniques described here, is misunderstood. For reasons of confidentiality examples from actual sessions are rare. The case studies explore some of the less publicized aspects of brainstorming, including the weaknesses of ideas when obtained in a training session as compared to the ideas obtained for a genuine client.

11.2 CASE STUDY 14: A DIVERSIFICATION EXERCISE WITHIN A SMALL FAST-GROWING COMPANY

The organization is a small but fast-growing firm producing and supplying commodities to specialist (trade) customers. In 1972, as part of a policy of continuous growth, the board set up a small group of managers to develop possibilities for new products in the short term (to achieve a significant impact on profits by 1975). The new-products groups which operated on a part-time basis, meeting approximately once a week, comprised technical, financial and commercial managers of ages ranging from early twenties to late forties. A management consultant was employed to introduce the principles of idea-generation techniques to the group, which at the same time hoped to be able to generate valuable ideas for new products. The meeting took place in an office of the client firm, equipped with flipcharts and easel for recording the ideas, tape recorder and writing materials. The consultant acted as leader; the liaison man who had contacted the consultant acted as client.

Orientation session

The subprocedures of the morning's brainstorming activities are shown in Figure 11:1. The orientation session took the form of a talk about the principles of creativity and idea-generation, illustrated with examples of creativity tests (Torrance 1962) and flexibility exercises (de Bono 1971). The group was encouraged to postpone judgement during the production of ideas, again as a preparation for the subsequent brainstorming exercise. Coffee was taken in conference toward the end of this session to avoid a break which might have reduced the value of the preliminary session. At this time a series of redefinitions (about a dozen) were produced, some splitting the

Figure 11:1 The subprocedures in the brainstorming session for new-product ideas

Subprocedure	*Time taken*
Orientation session: exercise to build trust and permit flexible speculative thinking	1½–2 hours
Redefinition of the problem (during coffee break)	5–10 minutes
Idea-generation practice session (using a sugar cube)	5 minutes
Brainstorming – after Osborn	10–12 minutes
Wildest ideas as starting points for original and practical insights	5 minutes
Individual brainstorming ('trigger sessions')	10 minutes
Individual development of ideas from other group members (6–3–5)	5 minutes

problem into subproblems; some redefining it through looking at it in a new way; and some adopting a metaphorical or speculative approach ('how can we print genuine pound notes for 50p each?'). During this redefinition stage attempts at evaluating the relative merits of the redefinitions were discouraged. It was pointed out that redefinitions of a complex problem can be obtained by examining it from different viewpoints and that, far from conflicting with each other, they illustrated different facets of the whole situation. The client was invited to nominate those redefinitions which presented the problem in a new light as far as he was concerned. He selected four redefinitions. These were used as starting points for the idea-generation stages which followed.

The leader explained that the final warm-up exercise before tackling the real problem was a form of practice brainstorming. The group members were reminded of the underlying principle of separating the idea-generation process from any evaluation or criticism stage. They were told that in order to minimize inhibitory criticism of their own ideas as well as those of the other group members, each person should be relaxed and be prepared to call out whatever ideas came into his head. The leader then asked the group to give as many uses as they could think of for a lump of sugar. (The item was selected arbitrarily as a common object that was at hand.) The first few ideas came hesitantly, were rather mundane, and none was speculative. The leader was able to increase the pace of production of ideas by setting up a rhythm, rather like a conductor of an orchestra, by repeating each idea and adding one or more ideas of his own to keep up the pace. After a minute, the group members were producing at a rate of one idea every three or four seconds, which indicated a reduced level of prejudgement by each individual. At this stage some ideas were highly speculative ('absorbs snake venom').

Afterwards the leader picked out instances within the exercise when group members had improved or developed on ideas, and asked for a similar effort during the subsequent brainstorming.

Idea-generation activities

The leader selected the most general of the redefinitions nominated by the client. This was written down on a sheet of the flipchart together with a précis of the principles on which the meeting was being conducted (see Figure 11:2).

Figure 11:2 Starting point for a brainstorming session – problem redefinitions and rules (after Osborn)

Problem redefinition: What extension of our services might our customers want?

RULES
Postpone judgement
Improve on ideas
Let ideas spark off new ideas

The message of Figure 11:2 was on view throughout the session. The leader then repeated the problem redefinition and the group began generating ideas which were all written on the flipchart and numbered sequentially by the leader.

He again attempted to increase the tempo of idea production which was, of necessity, rather slower than the warm-up exercise because each idea was being recorded manually on the flipchart. The leader did not introduce his own ideas, but relied for quickening the pace on asking idea-spurring questions like 'How can we do that? What else might do that? Can we combine the idea with any other?'

About 60 ideas were produced in 10 minutes. Although the group seemed to be postponing judgement, there were no very speculative ideas. The leader therefore let the tempo of idea production drop and then moved into a second variation of brainstorming based on the production of extremely speculative ideas (wildest idea – T.4.4). Each member of the group had to imagine a dream solution to the problem which disregarded the constraints of reality. The fantasy solutions were collected and written on the flipchart. Then each idea was briefly treated as a concept to be brainstormed until a realistic idea was developed. The results in one instance had a considerable positive impact on the client and other members of the group (to such a degree that the postponement of judgement principle was forgotten and the group began to develop the idea and how it should be progressed). The leader considered this a convenient time to introduce a further modification of brainstorming in order to progress the group away from a change towards an analytical attitude.

For the next exercise, a trigger session (T.4.2), each member of the group used the filing cards provided. The redefinitions obtained at the outset of the meeting were shared out among the group. Each member of the group was then instructed to carry out a sort of individual brainstorming on his problem redefinition, writing down his ideas in silence while trying to postpone judgement. A target of ten ideas with a time-limit of five minutes was set. After five minutes each member read out his ideas and attempted to generate a further set of ideas through the stimulation of the lists being read out. Approximately 40 ideas were produced in the first five minutes, and a further ten ideas were added in the second period. The most comprehensive and potentially valuable list of ideas was provided by the member of the group who had difficulty in cooperating and contributing to the meeting.

The leader explained that a further idea-generation session would normally be conducted using a second variation of individual brainstorming (6–3–5 or recorded round robin – T.4.3). He demonstrated the technique in extremely abbreviated form, so that the group would be able to use it in their own subsequent activities if they so desired. The session again started with each member selecting a redefinition of the problem or a subproblem and developing three possible broad solutions of different types, one on each of three cards. The cards were then exchanged among the group to permit modifications and improvements to all the ideas. Each improvement or modification was written underneath the original redefinition. Any completely new ideas sparked off were noted down on additional cards to be added to the final list. In the complete version of the procedure the 18 original ideas could have been modified five times, thus producing a minimum of 90 ideas. In this exercise only one exchange of ideas was carried out.

This concluded the first idea-generation session. Before leaving, the group noted those ideas which had appeared to have considerable potential and immediate applicability. Two such ideas were recorded. One had been generated in the first brainstorming session; the second came from one of the wildest ideas in the second exercise.

Evaluating and progressing the ideas

The ideas were evaluated initially by the member of the idea-generation team who had commissioned the meeting and who had most experience of the problem. He circulated a rough draft of all ideas produced to the participants. He also supplied them with a short-list of potentially valuable ideas obtained from the rough draft by a screening procedure which eliminated (*a*) wishful, vague, irrelevant and shallow ideas; (*b*) concepts which were the subject of current or past investigation and (*c*) those of low novelty and market potential. The other members of the original brainstorming group were to add to the short-list of any ideas which would pass through the screen after development or clarification of the original statement. Additional ideas occurring during this process were also added to the short-list if they passed the screening procedure. The liaison man then drew up a list of people who would be primarily concerned with the development and progress of the ideas through the organization. A meeting was arranged with these people at which time criteria for acceptance of new ideas were drawn up. The short-list had been circulated to these people before the meeting together with a request for further ideas which they felt should be added to the list. The first short-list contained approximately one dozen ideas, and a brief exercise was conducted by the client to evaluate each idea on financial, technical and organizational grounds. He was also able to build a prototype new product based on one of the new ideas.

11.3 CASE STUDY 15: AN EXAMINATION OF THE MATERIAL PRODUCED DURING A (TRAINING) BRAINSTORMING SESSION

The following brainstorming took place in half a day of a management course in 1970. The participants were trainee managers of various disciplines not experienced in brainstorming, assisted by three experienced practitioners. Before the brainstorming the group was introduced to the principles of creative problem-solving for about an hour.

Idea-generation sessions

The group separated arbitrarily into groups A and B, each with nine members (excluding the leader), to brainstorm the problem, 'improving the relationship between the British garage and the public'. Each subgroup spent five minutes in practice brainstorming the exercise, 'new uses for a brick', and then approximately half an hour on the actual problem. The ideas, as recorded at the time, are shown in Figure 11:3.

Figure 11:3 Examples of the output of a brainstorming session.
Unedited and in order of production

Brainstorming by group A
(Nine managers from a training course)

1 Leave old part in car.
2 Clean grease off car.
3 More uniform charging rates between garages.
4 Make sure item has been tightened up.
5 Guarantee the job.
6 Consult customer before further repairing.
7 Give a fair estimate at start of the job.
8 Have car ready on time.
9 Better uniforms for engineers.
10 Warm waiting room.

11 Respect for property.
12 Topless petrol-pump attendants.
13 Assistant to see car serviced.
14 An instant service.
15 Do-it-yourself garage.
16 Free advice.
17 Free loan of tools.
18 Adequate facilities.
19 Comprehensive spare-parts supply.
20 Clean car both inside and outside.

21 Full discount on all parts.
22 Stop gimmicks and cut prices on forecourt.
23 Better forecourt services.
24 All pumps under cover.
25 Good efficient service.
26 Instant part replacement.
27 Written estimates.
28 Open early on Sundays in summer.
29 Remain open later.
30 Rota system for 24-hour service.

31 Car loan while servicing.
32 Replace petrol cap.
33 Non-drip petrol.
34 Chart of charges at garage.
35 Know which mechanics are qualified.
36 Know who is the head mechanic.
37 More specialized garages: covering, for example, engines, body repairs, tyres, exhausts.
38 Inspector of repairs at garage.
39 Independent inspector of repairs.
40 Licence for insurance repairs and non-insurance repairs.

41 Stationary testing.
42 Proper washing days.
43 Engine washing days.
44 Efficient tyre-pressure check.
45 DOE government controlled.
46 Free forecourt antifreeze check.

Brainstorming by group B
(Nine managers from the same training course)

1 Improve workmanship.
2 More attention to staff quality.
3 Trusts.
4 Issue guarantees.
5 Tell you what they have done.
6 Make an honest estimate.
7 Trust reduction.
8 Improve training techniques.
9 Employee responsible for outcome of test.
10 Use good and correct materials.

11 Develop system technique for testing and servicing.
12 More accurate cost analysis.
13 Stand by estimate.
14 Attach equal importance to out and in inspection.
15 Don't overload day's work.
16 Senior or qualified people to pass vehicle.
17 Complete repair on date given.
18 Garages to be licensed.
19 Garages to lose franchise on repeated bad work.
20 Factory-trained mechanics.
21 Garages penalized for shoddy work.
22 Installation of up-to-date equipment.
23 Stand by the work they have done.
24 Guaranteed time work done and period for replacements.
25 Incentive payment to mechanics.
26 Full testing of vehicle after repair.
27 More frequent checks by AA and RAC.
28 Sales divorced from maintenance side of firm.
29 Carry sufficient spares to avoid delay.
30 Avoid civil-service control procedure – ie must be a man who can answer.

31 Security of vehicle while in their care.
32 Computer control.
33 Train management as well as staff.
34 Courtesy and advice given freely.
35 Prevent soiling upholstery from greasy overalls.
36 Lay down standard charges for standard work.
37 Accident damage has independent inspection from insurance company.
38 Attempt to repair damaged parts, not renew.

Figure 11:3 – continued

Brainstorming by group B – continued

39 Inform customer of faults found in any one job.
40 No false gimmicks.

41 Good advertising campaign.
42 Managers educated by manufacturers of new models.
43 Manufacturers insist on the prompt attention to mechanical failures under guarantee.
44 Cost to relate to parts, rather than the make of the car.
45 Reduction in costs for regular customers.
46 Advise if alternative parts can be fitted.
47 Correct inspection of tyres including pressures.
48 Complete breakdown of work done detailed on invoice.
49 Make good shoddy workmanship immediately.
50 Give more detailed accounts of labour costs.

51 Closer supervision by manufacturers.
52 Inspect and report to customer each 6 000 miles service.
53 Feed back information to manufacturers about ways of redesigning cars so as to reduce cost to consumer.
54 Feedback of information on frequently occurring faults.
55 More amenities to customers – tyres, windscreen washers, etc.
56 24-hour service, 7 days a week.
57 Overnight servicing and maintenance in densely populated areas.
58 Mechanics kept up to date.
59 Reduce time and costs.
60 Repair costs linked to insurance policies.

61 Guarantee period on completion of repair.
62 Have garage management more customer conscious to encourage business.
63 More competition between garages on price and quality of maintenance.
64 Mini-skirted receptionists.
65 Topless female mechanics.
66 Code of conduct and cost by *Which?*
67 Mechanic receptionists.
68 Satisfaction coupons.
69 Female accompaniment while vehicle being repaired.
70 Garage supporters' club.
71 Do-it-yourself service facilities.

Evaluation of the ideas

A colleague with experience of the garage trade classified the ideas according to level of speculation. Figure 11:4 indicates the changing levels of speculation estimated by him for successive batches of ideas produced.

11.4 CASE STUDY 16: BRAINSTORMING OF PROMOTIONAL IDEAS FOR A FOOD PRODUCT

A major manufacturer of retail food products tested the value of brainstorming by examining the results on one of its recurring needs – new ideas for giveaway items in a promotional campaign. The campaign was specified as one to promote a product selling through supermarkets with strong appeal to young people. The exercise took

Figure 11:4 *Level of speculation of ideas attained in a brainstorming session on the problem 'Improving the relationship between the British garage and the public'*

	GROUP A (46 ideas) Proportion of ideas with low, medium and high levels of speculation			*GROUP B* (71 ideas) Proportion of ideas with low, medium and high levels of speculation		
Ideas	*Low*	*Medium*	*High*	*Low*	*Medium*	*High*
1–10	7	3	0	6	4	0
11–20	7	1	2	6	4	0
21–30	10	0	0	2	5	3
31–40	8	2	0	5	4	1
41–50	6	0	0	5	4	1
51–60	–	–	–	6	4	0
61–70	–	–	–	5	0	5
71–80	–	–	–	0	1	0
Total number	38	6	2	35	26	10
Percentage	83	13	4.3	49	37	14

place in 1970 with a group made up of four members of a specialist new-products group skilled in brainstorming, and two marketing executives who wished to evaluate the technique. A warm-up session of approximately half an hour was followed by three-quarters of an hour of brainstorming of the Osborn type on the subject, 'giveaway items for our product'. The pace of idea production was furious, and the leadership changed halfway through, but without influencing the flow of ideas. Over 300 ideas were produced, samples of which are shown in Figure 11:5. In general the level of speculation was high (see especially ideas 291–300) and development of ideas occurred, sometimes subtly (140–2, and 290–3).

Figure 11:5 Ideas generated by brainstorming on the topic 'new give-away items'

Ideas 1–10	Sweets, chewing gum, Sellotape, glue, model kits, spillikins, small games, personal horoscopes, horror pictures, money
Ideas 41–50	Paper, face mask, balloons, car shampoo, map, key ring, car ring, ring, instant fish, birthday stamps, sachet of instant coffee
Ideas 91–100	Jigsaw puzzle, dice, cards, five stones, hairbrush, square marbles, hair colourant, nail scissors, nail file, nail varnish
Ideas 140–150	Door plates, door knocker, party rosette, gramophone needle, false teeth, funny noses and teeth, (censored), box of matches, matching boxes, match boxes, decimal calculator.
Ideas 191–200	Tea bags, knuckledusters, pendant, nail brush, child's drum, Sir Malcolm Sargent's conducting baton, torches, paper pads, curlers, rare leaves
Ideas 241–250	Sandwich boxes, toy bricks, dog biscuits, trouser presser, biscuit tins, hammer, toothpaste holder, *Radio Times* holder, picnic utensils, letter holder
Ideas 291–300	[290: religious things] *, miracle kit, conjuring kits, edible paper for secret messages, animal shampoo, good resolutions, aphrodisiac, dusting kit, car stickers, body transfers, zip or lock
Ideas 320–329	Car stickers, nail cutters, potato peeler, can opener, shaving cream, after shave, magnetic egg-timer, magnetic strip for many purposes, keep-fit wheel, pacifier.

*Idea 290 has been included to illustrate how a speculative idea can spark off others – eg, 291, 292, 293, 295.

11.5 CASE STUDY 17: BRAINSTORMING TO IMPROVE THE EFFICIENCY OF A CONTRACT RESEARCH ORGANIZATION

In 1972 a contract research organization held a seminar for R and D managers among its clients. One of the activities was brainstorming, and the topic selected was 'means of increasing the efficiency of this unit'. The director of the unit acted as client and he and the lecturer were the only two representatives of the unit present.

Fifty-five ideas were produced by Osborn's methods in 10 minutes. The group had spent approximately two hours before the ideas session discussing creativity, individual and group problem-solving. The director showed interest in implementing some of the suggestions, and after the seminar the list was circulated to eight members of the contract research organization with appended instructions:

> The following are the results of a brainstorming session. You may be interested in having a look at the ideas and perhaps commenting or improving on them. If you will eliminate the nonsensical ideas and indicate:
>
> 1 Ideas worth following up.
> 2 Ideas that suggest new concepts worth following up.
>
> I'll collect and collate them for later discussion. (In a brainstorming session up to 80 per cent of the ideas may be speculative or irrelevant.)

The results (Figure 11:6) show the variety of opinions that exists even within a compact and homogeneous unit of this type.

Implementation of the results

The most-favoured ideas were 'better public relations' (Idea 3) and 'more group activities' (Idea 22). In the next general meeting of the unit two actions were decided on – apparently independently of the brainstorming exercise. Two subcommittees were set up (thus increasing the level of group activity); one of them considered the visibility of the unit to its potential clients, and means of improving its image.

Figure 11:6 *Evaluation of ideas produced in a brainstorming session.*

The 55 ideas were produced in a short training exercise. They were suggestions for improving the efficiency of a contract research organization made by a group of outsiders, but evaluated by the eight senior staff within the organization.

Note. (*a*) the virtual impossibility of obtaining a conclusive ranking. (*b*) individual variation in perceptiveness or cooperation on the part of the evaluators. Within three months two study groups had been set up to examine the points covered in ideas 3 and 22 (the most favoured), although the impetus for the study groups came after a general meeting. (Reinvention phenomenon?)

Ideas

Assessors	1	2	3	4	5	6	7	8	9	10	11	12	13	14	15	16	17	18	19	20	21	22	23	24	25	26	27	28	29	30	31	32	33	34	35	36	37	38	39	40	41	42	43	44	45	46	47	48	49	50	51	52	53	54	55
1			●																																																	○ ●	●	●	●
2		●	●		●	○			○		○				○	●	○			○	○	●	○		○	●			●	●	○		○				○	○	○		○		●	○		○						○	○	●	○
3																○		○	●		●	●	○		●					●	●								○				○									●			
4			●	●	●	○	●	●	●		●				●	●	●		●	●	○	●	●		●	●		●	●	●	●	○	●	●		●	●		●		●		●	●		●	●					●	●		●
5		●	●	●	●	○										●					○	●	○						●	●	○ ●	○	●			●	●	●	○				●									●	●	●	●
6		○	○	●	●	●		○ ●		●		○			○ ●						●	●		●	○ ●	●				●			●			●					●		○							●			●		
7		○ ●	●					○							●	●	●					●	●								●					○																			
8		●	●	●	●	○		●						○								○		●	●	○					○						○	○								○							○	○	

KEY ● Ideas worth following up ○ Ideas suggesting more realistic concepts

11.6 CASE STUDY 18: RENT-A-BRAINSTORMING (HOLLAND)

In 1969 a rent-a-brainstorming service was initiated by a market research organization in Holland. Its objective is to provide industrial firms with solutions to problems of various types, using brainstorming sessions as the method of producing the ideas.

The overall problem-solving system is in three stages: fact-finding, idea-generation and solution-finding. In the fact-finding stage, the professional consultants work with members of the client organization defining the problem and preparing it in a format which is circulated to the people who will be involved in the brainstorming.

Format of the brainstorming

A permanent core of people for the brainstorming activity is provided by the company from the ranks of its market research executives. In addition it has built up a large panel of freelance brainstormers whose participation is restricted to evening sessions. These include mechanics, a masseur, a graphic designer, a journalist, a student, an officeworker, salesgirls, housewives and a works manager. Because of the large panel of freelance participants the company can arrange for a regular supply of fresh participants for groups. By a deliberate policy decision teams are not permitted to remain together for too long. A typical brainstorming group includes one or two members of the client organization involved in the problem, and full-time and freelance participants to make a total of between eight and eleven people. Using an Osborn-type procedure, the actual idea-generation process never goes on for longer than an hour, and approximately 100 ideas are produced.

Development of ideas

The entire output of the brainstorming session is circulated to the client without any screening by the market research organization. At first this practice proved a mistake due to unfavourable responses from clients who did not expect to receive quite such a mixture of speculative and down-to-earth concepts. As a consequence the output is now accompanied by a memorandum indicating how the ideas can be classified and evaluated.

11.7 NOTES ON CASE STUDIES 14–18

The majority of the groups were composed mostly of inexperienced participants. This did not lead to any diminution of performance as far as can be observed.

The actual output of the sessions recorded in Figures 11:3 and 11:5 are offered to the reader as an opportunity for analysing them and comparing with efforts with which he is personally involved. These are typical rather than inspired sessions, which should not detract from their value.

The following points are worth noting:

1 The changing level of speculation which occurs as the meeting proceeds. This is discussed in Section 5.4. Typically there is a peak towards the beginning of a session, sometimes followed by a larger peak associated with genuine integrative efforts on the part of group members.
2 The ideas produced by 'hitchhiking' – or random stimuli from one member's contribution influencing the ideas of another member of the group.
3 The length of the responses. Excessive length is indicative of conscious evaluation and justifications.

The Dutch group (Case Study 15) shows how a creative analysis of their procedure will improve results. Resistance to unexpurgated minutes of the sessions was recognized, and assistance offered to the client group during the evaluation process. This could have been strengthened by more attention to identification of the true agent and sphere of influence, and taking this into account in selection of the group members.

Chapter 12

Individual Open-ended Problem-solving

In this chapter several examples of individual creative problem-solving are presented, in technical, social, commercial and scientific contexts. With one exception the examples occurred during the period 1970–73.

12.1 CASE STUDY 19: CREATIVE THINKING APPLIED TO A SOCIAL PROBLEM

Michael Woods is an operational research scientist helping develop project evaluation and analysis systems within a large industrial organization. As part of his work he has introduced lateral thinking, brainstorming and synectics to reinforce more conventional methods of data collection and idea generation. He is very active in local politics in Bedfordshire, where he lives, and has applied his management skills to social and political problems.

In an article in the *Bedfordshire Times* (16 February 1972) Woods outlined the problem of decline of rural bus services in the Bedford area. In common with other commuter regions the villages are becoming increasingly dependent on car-owning residents. Urban services that visit outlying regions have longer and longer intervals between calls. As he pointed out:

A completely new approach is possible, particularly in Bedfordshire. The town (Bedford) is built like the hub of a wheel with spokes in the form of its main roads into the country . . . (see Figure 12:1). Our existing bus services spin a web about these spokes and finally arrive at the hub . . . Except for certain peak-hour journeys [a bus] travels nearly empty with the aim of filling steadily from its source [in Stevington] to its destination in the bus-station.

Our bus service is the wrong shape. A wishful but impossible dream of an ideal bus service would be an elastic bus that expanded as passengers got on. We would have a 6-seater, very cheap to run in Stevington; then a slightly dearer 12-seater by the time we got to Bromham, and a 20-seater at Biddenham.

Figure 12:1 *The elastic bus.*
The spokes of Bedfordshire's bus service. Current services (along spokes) could be augmented by minibus services linking the spokes and improving communications between outlying villages.

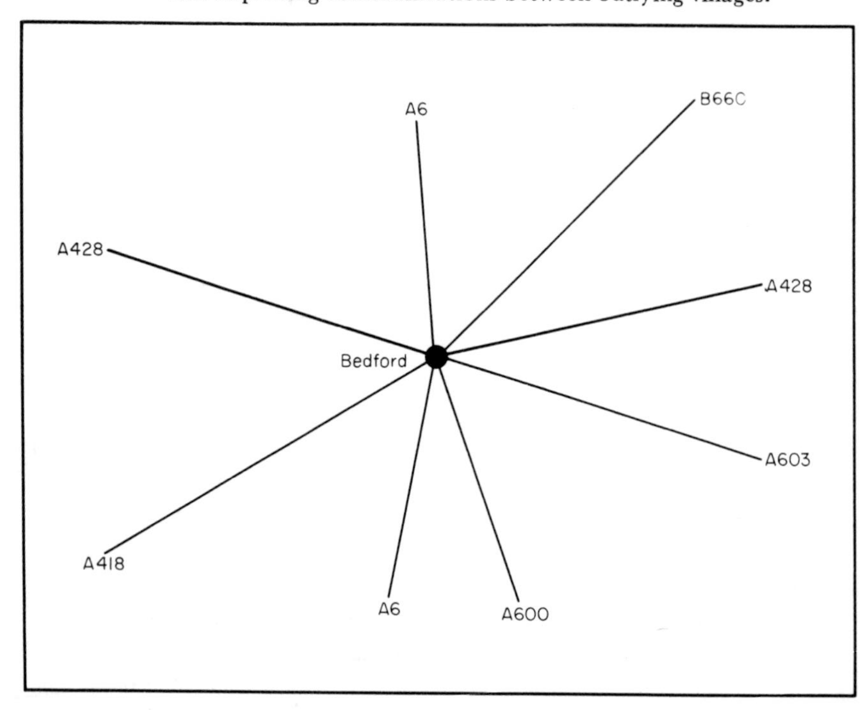

He added that such an impossible but desirable system would also permit passengers to travel directly to villages not on the main route.

> The impossible dream could be achieved by a complete rethink. Suppose our juggernaut commercial services travelled only on the spokes – the main roads leading into Bedford – during the offpeak periods. We have only the A6 service, the A418/B660, the A428 service and perhaps the A603 and A600 service. Now there's a different problem: how do we get passengers to the spokes and on to the juggernaut services? I suggest that we run an hourly minibus service in two orbital routes around Bedford. This service would pass through the bigger villages and deposit their passengers on the nearest 'spoke'. Because the orbital service is unlikely to be profitable I suggest this service is the council's direct responsibility. The existing companies could deal with the 'spoke' service as a commercial venture . . .
>
> The routes of the minibus could be complicated because no one would expect to be on the bus for any extended period. The bus could be fast because it is small and not the traffic danger of the double-decker. I suggest two orbital routes for all the villages, and a target of an hourly service. The spoke service could aim at a maximum of a half-hour wait, and all the spoke stops should be covered. A second generation of the system could be run in two directions . . .
>
> The experts will be able to find a thousand things they can criticize in the suggestion: cost, finding the drivers, reorganizing the routes on to peak and nonpeak conditions, insurance on the minibus, waiting periods on main roads, and (most important) that it has not been done before. My reply is that the old ideas for rural transport have been given a fair crack of the whip and have blatently failed. They are expensive and do not give the public a good service.
>
> The need is there, and is likely to increase. If you have a better idea Mr Expert, let's have it.

Examining his line of thought later, Woods remembered thinking to himself that a good 'intermediate impossible' for the bus service would be an elastic bus. He was then able to come down to reality very quickly through the transition step of a 6-seater becoming a

12-seater and then a 20-seater bus. The concept was accepted in principle by the opposition party of Bedford's Urban District Council.

12.2 CASE STUDY 20: INDIVIDUAL CREATIVITY LEADING TO TECHNICAL INNOVATION

In 1972 Mr Abdul Hameed Quraishi received the Technical Development Corporation/Guardian Innovator award – a prize of £5000 – for a new hollow-mould process for casting metals. Mr Quraishi was the initiator and managing director of a small family manufacturing business in Kettering, Northants. The company, formed in 1960, produces solvent cleaners, degreasing agents and a variety of plastic floor-covering materials.

His early life demonstrates resilience in the face of danger and misfortunes: as a chemistry student, his degree studies were interrupted when first Delhi University, and then the Punjab University in Lahore, had to suspend their courses in chemistry because of the partition riots of the 1940s. When he resumed his studies he turned to civil engineering, partly because the faculty was one of the few that were relatively intact in the area. He arrived in England as a cadet in the Royal Pakistan Navy at Dartmouth and specialized in electrical engineering, earning himself exceptional advances in seniority for his performance. He left the Navy, started his manufacturing business in 1960 and gradually acquired a reputation as an imaginative technical expert with a wide knowledge of protective coatings and plastics.

Preparation period

In the years 1969–72 his interest was turned to the problem of flammability of foamed plastics. The materials have excellent properties as insulators, and find wide application in the home for refrigerators and wall laggings. However, they tend to have rather poor resistance to heat, and can be extremely inflammable in the event of a domestic fire. The greater thermal stability of optional materials is offset by high costs, or considerable production complications.

Quraishi began a systematic study of the effects on the thermal properties of polymers of substituting different chemical groups. As well as testing chemical groups likely to lead to stability he also tested many which were likely to produce unstable products in order to learn more about adverse consequences. During this period he procured a large number of polymers with a variety of physical states and thermal stability. He arrived at a point at which he had tested several hundred materials without finding any of outstanding merit in satisfying his original objective.

Incubation period

At this crisis point in the project he was unable to forget his work on returning home. In view of the spectacular flammability of some of his materials he began to wonder whether there was an opportunity based on reasonably priced and easily processed plastics which burned very well. For some reason as he went to bed, he recalled the legend of the discovery of roast pork many centuries ago by a Chinese peasant whose cottage burned down with the family's pig still inside. While rummaging through the ashes the distraught peasant discovered the pig, roasted to perfection, and exceedingly edible.

Soon, all over China, cottages were being burned down with pigs left 'accidentally' inside.

Moment of inspiration

Quraishi eventually fell asleep, still thinking about the tale of the discovery of roast pork until, in his own words, 'I woke up from a dream muttering "pig iron . . . cast iron . . . Eureka!" '

Validation process

It was about four o'clock in the morning when he got up and began to work on the details, until in a few hours the outline of the new project was complete. He had invented an improved method of casting metal which utilized the flammability of his newly discovered plastic foams.

The first stage of the process involves production of a foam-plastic replica of any desired shape obtained by rotating a master copy on a moulding machine and permitting the plastic foam to assume the same shape through centrifugal force. The plastic mould can then be removed and inserted in a sand box and molten metal poured in. The hot metal burns up the easily combustible foam plastic which, during the exothermic reaction, is eliminated mostly as gaseous combustion products. The honeycomb nature of the foam has its own built-in supply of oxygen to support the reaction.

The invention has attracted considerable interest in Europe and America. Among the unique features claimed in the covering patents, is the use of foamed plastics of good exothermic properties (that is, highly combustible) as self-destructing moulds in the casting of metals.

Quraishi has always enjoyed inventing things – gadgets, a burglar alarm activated by the proximity of the human body, extensions to his firm's range of floor-covering materials, etc. When involved in a task he is driven to complete it – for example, he worked 48 hours non-stop to complete the preliminary patents of his foam-plastic moulding process.

12.3 CASE STUDY 21: INDIVIDUAL ENGINEERING CREATIVITY: BREAKAWAY ROAD STANDARDS

Between April 1963 and March 1964 over 200 people were killed on the roads of Great Britain in collisions with street-lighting columns. This figure represents about 5 per cent of all road deaths (excluding pedestrians) for the period. The Road Research Laboratory had been studying these problems for some years. One of the senior engineers allocated to the work, Mr R. L. Moore, became convinced of the need for an entirely new approach. The Laboratory was at the time studying a variety of new materials as possible lamp standards and road 'furniture'. While advantages over conventional columns were often demonstrated there were generally flaws which ruled out the use of the new materials with conventionally designed columns. At about this time Moore began to experience a recurrent form of vision of a solution. In his mind's eye, he saw a lamp column which would disappear on impact. He recalled discussing the problem with the manufacturers and describing his new approach to the problem as discovering a mechanism to permit the column to break away on impact. The manufacturers came up with a solution which involved filling the bottom 6 feet of the column with concrete. Although this solution could lead to the upper part of the column flying away, or to preserving the column on impact, it did nothing to alleviate the plight of the motorist running into one. The Road Research Laboratory continued its investigations.

Eventually a design was developed which performed as the columns in Moore's earlier fantasies. It was designed by P. W. Turner of the

Cambridge University Department of Engineering. It was based on a shear joint. The final design took into account the need to have a built-in weakness of a form which did not weaken the column to wind loads. The joint is shown diagrammatically in Figure 12:2. The joint is located about 3 or 4 inches from the base of the column and low enough to avoid fouling of the vehicle. The two portions are connected through welded flanges clamped with four bolts. On collision, the flanges slide apart, causing the bolts to tear the gasket separating them. At high speeds the top part of the column somersaults over the car to rest approximately in line with the direction of travel. When positioned as recommended by the code of practice for street lighting at a distance of more than 5 feet beyond the road boundary, the angle of impact with vehicles tends to be rather acute, and the fallen column remains off the main highway.

Figure 12:2 *A breakaway (weakened) joint.*
Simplified version of the joint as described by Walker and Hignett, Road Research Laboratory, in May 1967 issue of *Highways and Public Works.*

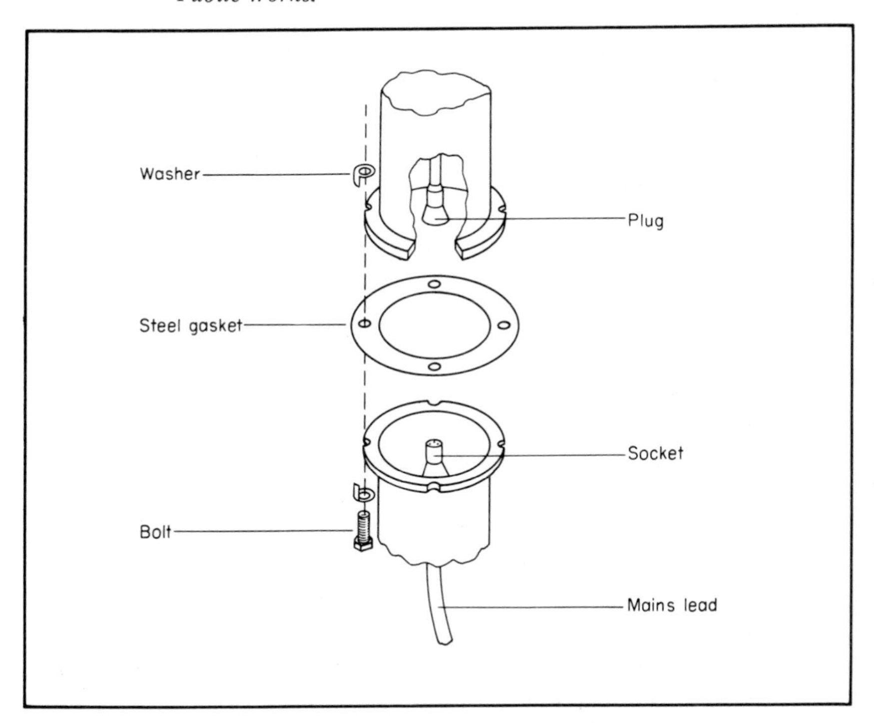

After considerable trials and modifications, the breakaway lighting column incorporating the shear joint was developed and patented throughout Europe. The design won an international prize in 1968 and has been taken up extensively in the USA following studies made in this country for the United States Bureau of Public Roads. Although the statistical evidence claimed by the Road Research Laboratory indicates that their innovation would save lives, there are as yet very few breakaway lighting columns in operation in the UK. Risks have been identified from the use of the columns as follows:

1 The falling shafts might endanger pedestrians and could be the cause of secondary accidents to following vehicles.
2 At low speeds the shaft of the column will fall onto the roof of the colliding car.

To counteract such objections, it has been pointed out that the columns could have real advantages under specific circumstances. These would be situations in which there are few pedestrians (motorways) and on roads carrying fast traffic where the majority of serious accidents are of the one-car type on the verges of roads. The columns should be sited on verges rather than central reservations.

A small number of stretches of road have been lit by lightweight columns in the UK. The results support the designers' theory of the safety features. From about 30 collisions to date only one serious casualty has occurred, and in that case the driver had already collided at high speed with two other vehicles before hitting the column. In about half the cases the driver had been able to drive his car away without reporting details of the incident. In the remaining cases for which information is available, only one person sustained any injury at all, but was not seriously hurt.

In one accident for which information is available one of the standards was hit by a bus travelling at approximately 15 miles an hour. The standard behaved as it was intended to and broke away to land on the verge. The Road Research Laboratory has photographs of the bus after the collision showing damage which could hardly be classified as more than minor scratches to the paintwork at the front. No injuries were incurred and some of the passengers were unaware that any accident had happened until afterwards.

12.4 CASE STUDY 22: CREATIVITY IN A BIOLOGICAL RESEARCH PROJECT

Mr Timothy Bagenal is a member of a biological research team examining the ecology of Lake Windermere. One of the problems he encountered was sampling freshwater larvae, and he eventually hit on a novel and improved procedure. The following account is in Mr Bagenal's own words as communicated to me.

> I had thought about the problems of sampling larval fish quantitatively for several years, while I was primarily working on other subjects. I decided that it ought to be the next subject to tackle (because the natural history of larvae is the biggest gap in our knowledge of fish), so I spent some time watching larvae and their reactions to nets of the type usually used to catch them. From the field observations I concluded that a successful quantitative net must:
>
> 1 Approach from below.
> 2 Work when the humans had gone and the shoals of larvae had settled down.
>
> Up to this stage I see the development as logical thinking.
>
> The next stage involved imagination and I tried to think of answers to the question, How can a net be made to rise from the bottom when I am not there to pull it up? Various ideas came to mind and were tried out. The first was that the net would have a bicycle tube ring which could be inflated through a pipe from an air cylinder several yards away on the shore. This did not work, and the trials showed that it never would. It was obvious that the ring had to be buoyant to start with and be held down by a weight with a release device. A net with a buoyant ring was easy to make, so the only problem was the release device. I discarded the idea of something clockwork or electronic as too expensive. The obvious answer seemed to be something that dissolved. I tried bags of sugar and salt but there were other objections to these. I tried drilling a hole through a large humbug but it cracked so I tried a Polo mint. It soon became clear that a Polo mint would not withstand a pulling

strain but would withstand compression – that is, the pull of a loop of string through a ring with half a Polo acting as a peg. While trying to find a small, hard object that would dissolve in water I sent my assistant to the local sweet shop to buy a quarter pound of all hard sweets. None were as good as Polos.

To summarize, I think that the posing of the right question required logical thought and that answering required creative thought. Much of my work has to involve logical thought, but I believe that I am more of a creative thinker. I much prefer devising ways of doing things and ways of analysing and presenting data, and writing up the results, rather than working at the bench.

12.5 CASE STUDY 23: INVENTION OF A NOVEL BUSINESS GAME, 'TOP RAT'

In 1972 Rick Johnson, a graduate student, submitted a dissertation to the Victoria University of Manchester in partial fulfilment for a degree in business administration. He had elected to study his own innovative behaviour over a period during which he had invented and helped market a business game. The following account is made up of extracts from his own notes.

The idea of executive progression, and the concept on which the game is based, was born out of frustration when I was working for a large and badly managed company. It seemed that the actions of various managers could be defined by their concern for doing the job, political manoeuvring and their need to survive. One in particular seemed to do nothing but play Machiavelli. There was another gentleman who was very talented at surviving; indeed, he seemed to survive to the extent of never entering into political intrigue or risking his career by doing some work. Every time this particular manager wrote a memo or attended a meeting, further evidence of his surviving tactics could be illustrated. Indeed, this soon became a joke among my colleagues. So, with considerable humour, the idea evolved of executives moving round a triangle which had at the three apices work, political manoeuvring, and surviving.

I thought at the time it would be possible to adapt this idea of executive progression into some form of game. It would be very amusing and also contain what I felt to be a relevant but cynical comment about managerial careers. However, I could not see a way of making it work in a simple and straightforward manner. Also, I considered that there was no possible hope of a commercial future as the whole thing seemed to be rather complicated. Yet, on the other hand, I believed the concept had some merit and would be of interest to other people. At its very early stage, I presented the idea to a number of colleagues who shared my frustration in working for this particular company, and it seemed to be well accepted. It is fair to say that this encouraged me to pursue the ideas. This initial stage occurred in May 1971.

From then until February 1972, development was static. However, I kept thinking of how to operationalize the idea into a game. In this period of eight months I had no particular motivation to try to force through the development, as I could see no way of taking it any further than deriving some satisfaction from making a novel idea more presentable. Anyway, I did not get anywhere towards making it into an attractive game. Indeed, I did not seem to have any feel or grasp of how it might work. Still, the idea kept nagging away and I wondered whether I could publish it as a general theory of executive progression in some magazine such as *Management Today*; I felt the readers might appreciate a somewhat offbeat approach. But the idea was not strong enough to get me to write it up in a formal sense.

From idea to an entertaining game

In March I began to think that it might really become something. However, I still did not know how to do it. I spent some time talking to friends at the Business School about the general theory of executive progression and, as with my previous company, the apparently frivolous idea got quite an interested reception. At this stage, the middle of the course, I was attending seminars on business and organization. My group was led by a successful entrepreneur. This, and lots of other little factors – such as wanting to make it work for its own sake and make a joke about 'models' of business – made it easy for me to give some time to roughing out ideas on how to make the idea into a game. At around this time the idea of selling a game idea to Waddingtons did present itself. In retrospect it seems that circumstances in March created the conditions to spur me on to following the idea through. However, I was still motivated by wanting to make it work just for its own sake, as I did not think that it had any commercial future because it seemed far too complex to be acceptable in a more general sense. Certainly the environment of the School and the style and jargon of the institution made it much easier to work on the idea than when I was in full-time employment.

At last the crucial idea came. It was to use the triangle to earn credits that would enable the player to move up on a hierarchy, the 'organogram'. Up to this stage all my thoughts had been directed at trying to make the idea into a game by playing it on just one board, the triangle, and for some reason which I cannot explain, I thought of playing it on two boards; from now on operationalizing the game was very straightforward, mainly a matter of trial and error. Even quite soon after I had operationalized the idea, I could not recall what made me think of playing it on two separate boards. Indeed, I could not see why I had not thought of this right from the start. It was an idea that just arrived. However, to the best of my knowledge, I do not know of another game of this type which is played on two separate boards. There was some difficulty working out the coordinate system on the triangle, but this was only because I could not see the wood for the trees. The idea of 'opportunity cards' came easily: it was an obvious adaptation of the use of chance cards which are common in many board games. At this stage in the development I drew various forms of organization charts to see which one would give the most interesting game. One aim was to postpone the outcome to the very last round.

Some conclusions

The successful development of 'Top rat' from the initial idea of management progression to invoicing the first customer appears to have been dependent on just five critical events:

1 Forming the idea that management action could be modelled by three interdependent variables: work, political manoeuvring and actions to ensure survival.

2 Operationalizing the idea into a game by seeing that it could be played on two boards, earning on one and progressing on the other.
3 Seeing that a possible commercial proposition existed if the *Manchester Evening News* gave the game as a Christmas gift to their customers.
4 The managing director of an advertising agency also seeing the *Evening News* opportunity and proposing to present the game.
5 The successful selling of the game by the managing director and myself.

All the other problems and difficulties were relatively minor compared to the above stages. I felt that, however serious they appeared at the time, the project was never at risk. However, if any of the above five had not proved soluble then the whole exercise would have failed. The two crucial moments were when:

1 The idea became a game and not just an assortment of interesting thoughts.
2 I discovered a possible commercial outlet when the agency managing director supported the proposal.

What conclusions can be drawn from this experience? First, circumstance contributed significantly to the successful outcome. It was very fortunate that the agency had as one of its clients the *Evening News*. Yet it was my own interest in business activities like advertising that caused me to seek work at an agency. A similar double influence brought the project forward from idea to game. It was the influencing environment of the Business School that crystallized my thoughts, but my own attitudes and aspirations that brought me to the School.

A second conclusion stems from the effect of having specific goals to work towards. My motivation was always low when there was no specific objective. It was easy to devote time and effort when:

1 The glimmering of an idea existed and it needed formalizing into a demonstrable theory of executive progression.

2 The concept of a game existed and it needed operationalizing into a playable party game.
3 I needed the first cost estimate.
4 The prospect was interested.
5 When the order was placed.

Yet between 1 and 2 and between 2 and 3 my interest was low. This was despite a romantic hope that it could eventually be sold. This was not enough, what was needed was always a feasibly achievable objective. I do not consider this to be a startling conclusion as setting objectives is generally accepted as a good thing. However, the size and strength of the 'good' has been clearly demonstrated in this particular case.

What about the particular conditions at the time of getting the major ideas? These were:

1 The idea of executive progression arising out of a trade-off between different activities.
2 Making it a playable game.
3 Thinking that the School of Graphic Design could help.
4 Realizing the best way to sell the game.

In general the ideas just came. However, it seems to be a consequence of living with the problem and surrounding oneself with helpful people and situations. Excellent familiarity with the problem meant that when the solution passed by, so to speak, I spotted it. It soaked, it cooked, and from somewhere came the solution. 'Eureka!' I had solved it. This was particularly so when I saw how best to sell the game.

12.6 NOTES ON CASE STUDIES 19–23

These studies can be compared with other recorded examples in the literature (see, for example, Vernon 1970). In each case, the new ideas became 'obvious' once they have been stated and implemented.

The people involved seem to be intuitively behaving in the way in which the techniques (try to) encourage us to behave. Compare, for example, techniques T.3.3, T.3.4, T.3.5, T.3.7 with Quraishi's and

Wood's problem-solving styles. Furthermore, judgement is postponed during the creative stages of problem-solving.

The studies also illustrate other aspects of the creative process discussed in the literature. Classical accounts of creativity, both artistic and scientific, emphasize four stages of preparation, incubation, inspiration and validation (cf. Case Study 20). The regularly successful creative individual has to have a personality which allows him to become involved and engrossed in a problem in the preparation stages, and which also sustains the motivational drive to validate the idea once it has been formulated. These personality traits must be added to any abilities to generate solutions as characteristics of the innovator. Thus track record is not a bad guide to potential future innovative or problem-solving ability. Just as fluency in creativity tests is one measure of a person's ability to tackle open-ended problems, so is fluency at implementing ideas a measure of his potential to produce the truly innovative product sooner or later.

PART THREE

APPENDICES AND BIBLIOGRAPHY

Appendix 1

Changes in Emphasis in Synectics Practice and a Glossary of Terms

A1.1 CHANGES IN EMPHASIS IN SYNECTICS PRACTICE

Because of the rapid changes and advances made in the last 15 years, many current practitioners may find the descriptions in Chapter 6 quite different from their own ideas about synectics. The main changes can be traced from Prince's introduction of behavioural mechanisms to provide a more group-oriented approach around Gordon's earlier procedures for stimulating individual creativity. The changes were made more confusing by minor changes in emphasis, accompanied by redefinitions of procedures and stages within meetings. These can be understood better by comparing the flow chart in Figure 6:6 to the earlier methods shown in Figure A1:1. The earliest approach considered the creativity-spurring devices central to the technique, an attitude illustrated by the name given to pre-excursion stages – 'the purge'.

As awareness of implementation of ideas grew, the excursion became less important and the technique became more client-oriented.

Groups should not follow trends unthinkingly, however. For invention groups, earlier methods might still be the best for their needs, while consultancy or service groups are more likely to be

Figure A1:1 *Flow charts of earlier synectics procedures.*
See Glossary at end of Appendix 1 for explanation of the terms.

1 1968–1969 Variation		*2 1971 Variation*	
Problem as given	Approximate times taken for each element	Expert outlines problem	Approximate times taken for each element
Analysis and explanation by expert	(30 min)	At the same time group suggests goals and possible solutions	(20–30 min)
Purge	(30–60 min)	Leader selects goal as start to excursion (1–3 steps)	(10–30 min)
Generation of problems as understood	(15 min)	Force-fit	(5–15 min)
Choice of problems as understood		Possible solutions	(5–10 min)
Excursion (3 steps)	(20–30 min)	Leader selects goals and repeats process if time permits	(20–60 min)
Force-fit	(5–15 min)		
Viewpoints on possible solution	(5–30 min)		
(Total meeting time 2½–3 hours)		(Total meeting time 2–2½ hours)	

highly client-oriented and would especially benefit from the more recent behavioural developments.

A1.2 GLOSSARY OF SYNECTICS TERMS

The most frequently used terms have been put together in a glossary. The terms associated with Gordon have been classified (G) and more recent terms (P).

It is hoped that many of these terms will be discarded as synectics becomes assimilated into normal problem-solving practice.

Analogy procedures. (G). The use of analogy and metaphor is believed to be central to the creative process. The earliest of Gordon's mechanisms attempting to make the creative state more frequent involved the use of metaphor.

Book title. (P). See 'symbolic analogy'. This optional name for a step in the excursion was given because a good symbolic analogy crystallizes the information being discussed in rather the same way that a book title can sum up what the book is all about.

Building (on ideas). (P). Any idea can provide a stimulus for fresh ideas. Synectics training encourages people to improve on ideas, either automatically, or through the use of structures such as 'spectrum', or 'itemized response'.

Client. (P). In synectics terms, 'client' may have an emphasis that will not correspond to the way it is defined in Chapter 1. Here, the client is the person who has been judged responsible for the problem being studied. He is the person who must eventually implement the suggestions. As synectics developed, the importance of the client became more and more recognized, and it has become one of the main tasks of a leader to help the client receive new insights into his problem from stimuli provided by the group.

Direct analogy. (G). A direct analogy is a straightforward comparison of two parallel facts or concepts from different environments. Thinking in terms of direct analogies has led to important technical and scientific discoveries. In synectics, the direct analogy stage of an excursion provides the group with an opportunity to think in such a manner. For example, when studying the problem of stopping leaks in bridges over motorways, the group may consider examples of leak protection from the world of nature. Examples produced (such as 'blood-clotting') may suggest valuable and original ideas.

Essential paradox. (P). See 'symbolic analogy'.

Examples. (G). One way of obtaining information during an excursion is to ask for examples relating to some concept which has been produced.

Excursion. (G). The part of a synectics session in which a group considers metaphorical relationships to a problem. An excursion may work by encouraging a period of incubation, permitting the subconscious mind to work on the problem, while the conscious mind considers something else. It may also aid the production of new insights because of the power of the metaphoric relationships in the creative process.

Expert. (G). In some cases the client is the person who has the most technical knowledge about a problem, and could be considered the expert. Recently the tendency is to play down the term as it implies a special status by virtue of expertise which should not exist in a correctly operating synectics group.

Feedback. (P). Training in feedback enables one member of the group to show another that he has understood what has been said. Feedback is essentially a communication and trust-building exercise.

Force-fit. (P). It is absolutely essential that any excursion is eventually channelled towards ideas that are relevant to the problem. The forcing of metaphorical speculative material towards realistic solutions has been termed the force-fit. It is one of the hardest parts of a synectics session to achieve. Considerable practice and self-confidence is required from group and leader to prevent a group from returning instantly to the problem, and thinking along lines similar to those produced before the excursion.

GAU (goal as understood). (G). An earlier term for individual redefinitions of the problem, as understood by different members of the group. (See PAU.)

Get-fired. (P). One mechanism to achieve a force-fit is for the leader to keep the speculative level high after an excursion, to help a gradual return to practical considerations. For a first stage he asks for a fantasy solution, which under different circumstances would put the proposer's job at risk. This 'get-fired' idea is taken and made gradually more realistic until a possible-solution is recognized by the client.

Goals. (P). New ways of looking at the problem. A whole variety of different types of goals arise in synectics sessions. Some paraphrase the problem, some interpret it, some deliberately turn it around on its head to provoke new insights, and others are extremely speculative or introduce fresh random material to the situation. The use of goal language reduces the need to ask questions which put the client in a defensive position.

Group fantasy analogy. (G, P). One method of producing material during the excursion is for the group to build up a single fantasy picture that is possibly, but not necessarily, related to an aspect of the problem. The fantasy scenario can be rather like a dream sequence in which everyday constraints are broken, and thus new ideas produced.

How-to statements. (P). Many goals begin with the words 'how to' (as in brainstorming). An alternative name for goals of this type is therefore 'how-to' statements.

Itemization. (P). Itemization refers to a systematic attempt at dealing adequately but not exhaustively with one item at a time in any meeting.

Itemized response. (P). In synectics, itemized response is a specific way of examining a concept. First the advantageous elements of it are examined and noted. Those aspects which at first sight may cause concern are then noted, but in terms of holes which have to be plugged or possibly new subgoals which have to be examined.

Listening. Synectics participants are trained in active listening. The main trick is to avoid being sidetracked by one's own intrusive thoughts while someone else is speaking. These should be jotted down briefly, so that you can return to concentrate on the speaker as rapidly as possible.

Motherhood statements. (P). There are sessions at which a series of possible solutions are produced, but which on examination turn out to be new ways of looking at the problem (goals) of an idealistic nature, which gain everyone's approval, but do not contribute greatly towards a policy of action. Classic motherhood statements are often produced by politicians, who are always in favour of improving the quality of life, a higher standard of living, democracy and so on.

'Order' of solutions. This is an English contribution which has helped in understanding how certain solutions are less useful than others. The order of a solution gives an indication of the degree of change and effort necessary to implement it. The higher the order, the more

the original redefinition has been validly modified during the synectics session. Clients naturally prefer first-order solutions and will tend to work on second- or higher-order ones only when no satisfactory first-order solutions have been obtained. For example, in the problem in Case Study 1 of monitoring grease effluent, a first-order solution would be modifications to existing monitoring mechanisms; a second-order solution would be a new pump design (the actual solution obtained); an even higher-order solution would be methods for eliminating the effluent in the first place.

PAG (problem as given). (G). The original problem definition.

PAU (problem as understood). (G). As members of the group examine the problem as given, they see it in their own individual ways. Such new ways of looking at the problem were originally called PAUs, but the term was later replaced with the term 'goals' or 'how-to' statements.

Paraphrasing a person's idea. (P). This can lead to more constructive group interactions. The person whose idea it was is less inclined to reintroduce it at a later stage, and the person paraphrasing is in a better position to understand what was really intended.

Personal analogy. (G). In the personal analogy stage of an excursion, members of the group try to imagine what it feels like to be the object or part of the object under consideration. When a high level of identification takes place, the results are evocative and prove to be useful stimuli for deeper understanding of the concept. The exercise also seems to have a cohesive effect on group interactions. Most successful demonstrations of personal analogy steps have arisen when the problems are of an engineering, or design nature.

Possible solutions. (P). When first practising synectics it is often difficult to distinguish between new ways of looking at the problem (goals) and possible solutions to the problem. If there is uncertainty, then the statement is almost certainly a goal. The key characteristic of a possible solution is that it is easily testable by the client. Three questions may be asked, as a check. They are:

1 Is it novel? (In the sense that it has not yet been tried, rather than it has not yet been thought of by the client.)
2 Will it solve part (or all) of the problem if it works?

3 Can you see some critical actions which could validate or disprove it, and which could be implemented fairly rapidly?

The three factors could be summed up as novelty, relevance, and testability.

Purge. (G). In the early synectics experiments when the excursion was considered central to most meetings, any ideas produced before the excursion were considered likely to be less valuable than ideas produced afterwards. It became customary to spend a considerable time collecting the pre-excursion ideas so that they would not intrude on the more original ideas produced later. The attitude towards the earlier ideas can be assessed by the selection of the word purge to describe procedure. It became recognized, however, that the synectics procedure could generate extremely valuable insights without an excursion, partly because of the behavioural elements introduced and partly because the group is selected to provide a variety of background experiences. Because of this, valuable ideas may arise rapidly and should be treated with equal respect regardless of when they are generated. For this reason the term 'purge' dropped out of the synectics vocabulary.

Spectrum. (P). The spectrum policy sums up an attitude of mind. Any ideas should be regarded as having a spectrum of elements ranging from very good to very bad. A positive effort is made to examine the good points first, and then to treat weaknesses as elements which must be overcome. The spectrum policy later evolved into itemized response (q.v.).

Symbolic analogy. (G). The symbolic analogy stage is one subroutine which can be included as part of the excursion of a synectics session. The group members attempt to sum up the concept under discussion in an evocative way. The phrase preferably expresses the essence of the problem in an original way, often containing an element of paradox. The symbolic analogy was also known as a book title, or essential paradox. Examples of symbolic analogies are given in Case Study 1.

Synectics. A recent dictionary definition (Chambers 20th Century) is 'the study of processes leading to invention, with the end aim of solving practical problems, especially by a synectics group, a miscellaneous group of people of imagination and ability but varied interests'. The term was almost certainly reinvented by William Gordon to describe techniques which he developed together with George Prince. The term implies the bringing together of elements which were previously unrelated.

Vacation. (G). Another term for an excursion. During this part of the session the conscious mind gets away from all its concerns about the problem, permitting a period of incubation at a subconscious level.

Viewpoints. (G). Another name for a possible solution (q.v.).

Appendix 2

A Selection of Organizations with Interests Relevant to Creative Analysis

Organization	*Postal Address*	*Interests*
A.P. (The Association of Humanistic Psychology)	57 Minster Road, London NW2	Creativity
Abraxas Management Research	2 Kingston Road, New Malden, Surrey KT3 3LK	Synectics (UK licensees of Synectics Inc.)
Biofeedback Systems Ltd	5 Gordon Place, Withington, Manchester 20	Electronic measurement of creativity (EEG machines, etc.)
The British Institute of Management (BIM)	Management House, Parker Street, London WC2B 5PT	Management education and training
The CEI Creativity Working Party	Institution of Mechanical Engineers, 1 Birdcage Walk, London SW1H 9JJ	Development of creative ability

Organization	*Postal Address*	*Interests*
Nuffield Centre for Health Services Studies	Dr R. Gourley, Clarendon Road, Leeds L52 9PL	Creativity in medical and public health fields
The Creative Problem-Solving Institute	1300 Elmwood Ave, Buffalo, NY 14222, USA	Creativity training, brainstorming
HTS Management Consultants Ltd	Management Training Centre, Lane End, High Wycombe, Buckinghamshire	Psychological testing, seminar programmes on group dynamics and management development
INCA (Innovation through Creative Analysis)	The INCA Research Programme, Manchester Business School, Booth Street West, Manchester M15 6PB	Creative analysis in management training and new-product consultancy
Innovation and Development	6 Greek Street, London W1V 5LA	Creation and development of new-product concepts
Interface	P.O. Box 28, Wilmslow, Cheshire SK9 2JU	Group dynamics, rational and intuitive problem-solving
Matchett Training	14 Montrose Avenue, Redland, Bristol, BS6 6EQ	Executive development
NFER Publishing Company	2 Jennings Buildings, Thames Avenue, Windsor, Berkshire SL4 1QS	Psychological test materials

Organization	*Postal Address*	*Interests*
Synectics Inc.	G. Prince, 28 Church Street, Cambridge, Mass. 02138, USA	Synectics
Synectics Learning Systems	W. J. J. Gordon, 121 Brattle Street, Cambridge, Mass. 02138, USA	Synectics
Warren Lamb Associates	Westmorland House, 127–131 Regent St, London W1R 7HA	Management team planning and executive assessment

Bibliography

The reader has been asked to take a lot for granted regarding techniques and underlying principles. In fact the whole subject is excitingly open to debate and any manager wanting to make up his own mind will find the following key references of value.

Popper (1968) discusses open and closed systems; Vernon (1970) summarizes changing ideas about creative and analytical thinking and includes a paper on Guilford's three-dimensional model of cognitive skills. Koestler (1964) and Beveridge (1950) are also lucid and thought-provoking. The importance of redefinition in open-ended problem-solving seems to me to be implied in Kelly's personal construct theory as outlined by Bannister and Fransella (1971) and by Dunckler (1926), and the significance of people as stimuli is discussed in a body of literature dealing with communications and the transfer of technology (for example, Gruber and Marquis 1969).

The characteristics of the problem-solving agent have been taken from Prince's work on synectics (1970) and practical observations. 'Blocks' to creativity have been enumerated by various writers generally based on empirical groups (see, for example, Haefele 1962). The importance of separating analytic and creative techniques, while permitting them to interact has been described as one of the reasons for developing structural aids to creativity (Stanford Research Institute 1969).

The basic techniques seem in many cases to be described more often than they have been practised, the most comprehensive general account being given by Jantsch (1967). Osborn's *Applied Imagination* (1949, etc.) not only outlines his most memorable contribution to the subject – brainstorming – but gives general principles of open-ended problem-solving that anticipate later studies of motivational psychology. The coauthors of synectics have produced the only convincing books on that subject – Gordon's work (1961) dealing mainly with the creativity-spurring aspects, and Prince (1970) adding behavioural elements. De Bono (1971) summarizes his work on lateral thinking.

Two excellent books dealing with decision-making are by Kepner and Tregoe (1965) and Maier (1963). Morphological analysis is described mathematically by Zwicky (1948) and popularly by Allen (1952).

In addition almost every volume of the *Journal of Creative Behaviour* (USA) and *R and D Management* (UK) provide fresh ideas relating to creativity and managerial problem-solving.

In the following list the key references have been marked.

*Allen, M. (1952) *Morphological Creativity*, Englewood Cliffs NJ: Prentice-Hall

Andrus, R. (1968) 'Creativity: A function for computers or executives', *Journal of Marketing*, April, Vol. 32, No. 2

Bales, R. E. (1959) *Small Group Theory*, New York: Harper & Row

Bannister, D. and Fransella, F. (1971) *Inquiring Man*, Harmondsworth: Penguin

Benson, B. F. (1957) 'Let's toss this idea up' *Fortune*, October

Beveridge, W. I. B. (1950) *The Art of Scientific Investigation*, London: Heinemann

Clark, C. H. (1958) *Brainstorming*, New York: Doubleday

Davies, D. G. S. (1970) 'Research Planning Diagrams', *R & D Management*, Vol. 1, No. 1

*De Bono, E. (1971) *Lateral Thinking for Management*, New York: McGraw-Hill

Dunckler, K. (1926) 'A Qualitative Study of Productive Thinking', *Journal of Genetic Psychology*, Vol. 33, 642–708

Farris, G. F. (1972) 'The Effect of Individual Roles on Performance in Innovative Groups', *R & D Management*, Vol. 3, No. 1, pp. 23–29

*Gordon, W. J. J. (1961) *Synectics – The Development of Creative Capacity*, New York: Harper & Row

Gruber, W. H. and Marquis, D. G. (eds) (1969) *Factors in the Transfer of Technology*, Cambridge Mass: M.I.T. Press

Guilford, J. P. (1970) 'Creativity: retrospect and prospect', *Journal of Creative Behaviour*, Vol. 4, No. 3

*Haefele, J. W. (1962) *Creativity and Innovation*, New York: Reinhold

Hinricks, J. R. (1961) *Creativity in Industrial Scientific Research*, A.M.A. Bulletin No. 12

Hubert, J. M. (1970) 'Project Selection – R and D and the Company's Requirements', *R & D Management*, Vol. 1, No. 1

*Jantsch, E. (1967) *Technological Forecasting in Perspective*, O.E.C.D., Paris

*Kepner, C. and Tregoe, B. (1965) *The Rational Manager*, New York: McGraw-Hill

Koestler, A. (1964) *The Act of Creation,* London: Hutchinson

Kuhn, T. S. (1970) *The Structure of Scientific Revolutions*, second edition. Chicago/London: University of Chicago Press

Langrish, J. *et al.* (1972) Wealth from Knowledge – A Study of Innovation in Industry, London: Macmillan Press.

Machiavelli, N. (1513) *The Prince*, (Translated by F. C. Bell, 1961.) Harmondsworth: Penguin

*Maier, N. R. F. (1963) *Problem-solving Discussions and Conferences*, New York/London: McGraw-Hill

Management Training Ltd (1971) *Creative Thinking and Brainstorming*, (Audio-visual programme.) London: Management Training Ltd

*March, J. G. and Simon, H. A. (1958) *Organizations*, New York: Wiley

*Maslow, A. H. (1954) *Motivation and Personality*, New York: Harper & Row

Medawar, P. (1967) *The Art of the Soluble*, London: Methuen (1969. Harmondsworth: Penguin)

*Osborn, A. (1957) *Applied Imagination*, New York: C. Scribner & Sons

Pessemier (1966) *New Product Decisions*, New York: McGraw-Hill

*Popper, Sir Karl (1968) *The Logic of Scientific Discovery,* third edition. London: Hutchinson

*Prince, G. (1970) *The Practice of Creativity*, New York: Harper & Row
Rickards, T. (1973) 'Brainstorming in an R and D Environment', *R & D Management*, Vol. 3, No. 3
Rogers, C. (1961) *On becoming a Person: A Therapist's View of Psychotherapy*. Boston Mass: Houghton Mifflin/London: Constable
*Sampson, P. (1970) 'Can Consumers Create New Products?' *Journal of the Market Research Society*. Vol. 12, No. 1
*Schon, D. (1969) *Innovation and Evolution of Ideas*, London: Tavistock Publications
*Stanford Research Institute (1969) *Structural Approach to Creativity*, Report No. 385
*Torrance, E. P. (1962) *Guiding Creative Talent*. Englewood Cliffs NJ: Prentice-Hall
*Vernon, P. (ed) (1970) *Creativity – Collected Readings*, Harmondsworth: Penguin
Wertheimer, M. (1945) *Productive Thinking*, New York: Harper & Row
Woods, M. F. and Davies, G. B. (1972) *Decision Design and the Computer*, Institute of Chemical Engineering, Symposium Series No. 35
*Zwicky, F. (1948) *Morphological Creativity*, New York: Interscience

Index

The words in italics are differentiated to indicate a specific connotation in the context of this book